Theodore S. Van Dyke

Millionaires of a Day

An inside History of the great southern California

Theodore S. Van Dyke

Millionaires of a Day
An inside History of the great southern California

ISBN/EAN: 9783743331181

Manufactured in Europe, USA, Canada, Australia, Japa

Cover: Foto ©ninafisch / pixelio.de

Manufactured and distributed by brebook publishing software (www.brebook.com)

Theodore S. Van Dyke

Millionaires of a Day

Millionaires of a Day.

Books by Theodore S. Van Dyke.

"That prince of sportsmen, T. S. Van Dyke."—*Sacramento* (Cal.) *Bee*.

SOUTHERN CALIFORNIA.

Its Valleys, Hills, and Streams; Its Animals, Birds, and Fishes; its Gardens, Farms, and Climate. 12mo, Ex. Clo., beveled, $1.50.

"May be commended without any of the usual reservations."—*San Francisco Chronicle*.

THE STILL HUNTER.

A Practical Treatise on Deer-Stalking. 12mo, Ex. Clo., beveled, $2.00.

"The best, the very best work on deer hunting."—*Spirit of the Times* (N. Y.)

"Altogether the best and most complete American book we have yet seen on any branch of field sports."—*New York Evening Post*.

RIFLE, ROD and GUN in CALIFORNIA.

A Sporting Romance, combining the interest of a novel with authoritative descriptions of the hunting and fishing in a country celebrated among sportsmen.

"Crisp and readable throughout, and at the same time, gives a full and truthful technical account of our Southern California game, afoot, afloat, or on the wing."—*San Francisco Alta California*.

FORDS, HOWARD, & HULBERT,
NEW YORK.

Millionaires of a Day:

AN INSIDE HISTORY

OF

THE GREAT SOUTHERN CALIFORNIA

"BOOM."

BY

T. S. VAN DYKE,

AUTHOR OF "THE RIFLE, ROD AND GUN IN CALIFORNIA," "THE STILL
HUNTER," "SOUTHERN CALIFORNIA."

NEW YORK:
FORDS, HOWARD & HULBERT.
1890.

COPYRIGHT, IN 1890,
BY
THEODORE S. VAN DYKE.

PREFACE.

"I WOULDN'T have missed it for all I have lost. It was worth living a lifetime to see."

So said to the author last year one of the ex-millionaires. And in truth he was not far from right. One who has not, as an actor, been through a first-class "boom" has missed one of the most interesting points of view of human nature.

Now that we have had plenty of time to look back upon the great boom that raged so long in the six southern counties of Southern California and gauge its immensity, we can see that it had never its like on earth. There have indeed been times of wilder excitement, when property has changed hands oftener in twenty-four hours and brought perhaps higher prices, but they were limited to a single point or to a brief period, and nearly always to both. But this boom (for convenience we will drop the quotation-marks hereafter) lasted nearly two years, embraced a vast area of both town and country, and involved an amount of money and players almost incredible to even those who were in it.

There was nothing in this analogous to any South Sea Bubble, or oil or mining stock swindle, or any other of the great humbugs of the past. The actors in this great game were not ignorant or poor people, and from end to end there was scarcely anything in it that could fairly be called a swindle. What few misrepresentations there were, were mere matters of opinion such as no one of sense ever relies on, any more than he does on the assurance that he will double his money within so many days. With a very few exceptions the principal victims were men of means. Most of them, and certainly the most reckless of them, were men who in some branch of business had been successful. Very many of them were "self-made men" who had built up fortunes by their own exertions, and were supposed to know right well the value of a dollar, and to have some idea of the value of property. All had the amplest time to revise their judgments and investigate the conditions of the game. The country all lay open, was easily and quickly traversed, and the advantages or disadvantages of any point could be readily seen. Over and over again the shrewdest of them did revise their judgments, debated with themselves the question whether they were fools or not, and the more they debated the more they were convinced that they were underestimating instead of overestimating the situation. And some of the silliest of the lot were men who, during the first three fourths of the excitement, kept carefully out of it, and did nothing but sneer at the folly of those who were in it.

The history of such a craze seems worth writing. Much has, of course, been told about it; but no one, unless he had a hand in it and could see its inside working, can tell of it in its most important phases, and nothing would be history that did not follow the results of the folly to their end.

To the people of the older States much of this will seem mere burlesque, and they will toss it aside as unworthy of belief. But the Californian will say that instead of being an exaggeration many interesting facts have been suppressed, probably because the writer dare not tell them. But enough has been told to interest all who were in it, though it will awaken many a painful recollection, and enough to warn any one who will study it from ever gambling on a margin on any prospects, no matter how good a judge he may think himself of booms and conditions of growth. Of course no warning will have any effect upon the great majority; but one thing is certain—the Californians want no more booms. A steady and substantial growth they do want, are having now, and will continue to have if Eastern boomers do not again set them crazy. They want nothing that will again check true development as the great boom did, and will advise all who think of coming to California to read this brief sketch of the greatest piece of folly that any country has ever seen.

SAN DIEGO, CAL., September, 1890.

CONTENTS.

CHAPTER I.
SOUTHERN CALIFORNIA BEFORE THE BOOM, . . 7

CHAPTER II.
THE CHANGES OF TEN YEARS, . . . 23

CHAPTER III.
THE BEGINNING OF THE BOOM, ... 38

CHAPTER IV.
THE SHEARING OF THE LAMBS, . . , 56

CHAPTER V.
THE SMILE OF THE NATIVE, . . . 82

CHAPTER VI.
AND AGAIN THE NATIVE SMILES, ... 95

CHAPTER VII.
HIGH TIDE OF THE BOOM, ... 105

CHAPTER VIII.
Getting Out, ... 130

CHAPTER IX.
The Collapse, ... 145

CHAPTER X.
The Overloaded, ... 154

CHAPTER XI.
Turning Over a New Leaf, ... 168

CHAPTER XII.
The Falling of the Roses, ... 177

CHAPTER XIII.
The Ex-Millionaire's Opinion, ... 195

Millionaires of a Day.

CHAPTER I.

SOUTHERN CALIFORNIA BEFORE THE BOOM.

From 1870 to 1875 Southern California was passing out of the control of the large land-owners, nearly all of whom were raising cattle, horses, and sheep to the exclusion of everything else, and into the control of the general farmer and fruit-grower. These were mainly small owners of what had been public land. Some of the great ranchos or Mexican grants, which embraced the greater part of what was then considered good land, had been opened by the owners to settlement. But most of the large owners were unwilling to injure their stock-range by admitting scattering farmers; so that the great majority of the new settlers were upon the outlying tracts of public land around the edges of the large ranchos, and in the small pockets and valleys of the surrounding hills. In 1875 their number was considerable; but their work was a combination of laziness, imitation of Mexican methods, and general shiftlessness, the bad effects of which were increased by ignorance of the peculiarities of California.

Almost every attempt of this class to make a dollar from the soil was thwarted by these causes, and in most cases it was impossible for the "granger" even to support his family in anything like comfort. Hundreds lived for a while on the little money they had brought here, then on credit until it swept away the farm, when they went to a new piece of government land to repeat the same folly. Nevertheless there was an attraction about the soft climate of winter and the dry, cool sea-breeze of summer, in the long line of sunny days with nights made for soundest sleep, and in the absence of storms, high winds, and other climatic discomforts, that made people stay, however unsuccessful, and steadily brought more to stay with them. It was a grand play-country, and one could get along with less than in any other part of the United States and still be respectable and fat. But everywhere there was a broad smile when some enthusiastic new-comer said that it would some day be the richest part of the United States outside the great cities.

Descending one day in the fall of 1875 from a hunt among the foothills of one of the great mountain ranges of Southern California, my companion and I came into a little valley or pocket where one of the long slopes of a great valley broke into the hills. It contained some sixty acres of dark soil along the bed of a little creek, with some reddish land sloping toward the hill on one side. The bottom-land looked as if with judicious coaxing it might be induced to raise a bean or possibly a cabbage; but nothing could seem more hopeless than any attempt to raise anything on the land that sloped toward the hills.

The most conspicuous thing about the place or "ranche," as all such places were then called, was a group of some two hundred bee-hives set upon low stands on a bit of rising ground at the base of the hill. Around some of them a few bees were lazily crawling, but the greater number of hives were silent. Near by was the "honey house," also deserted, except where a few bees were exploring the key-hole and the chinks in the sides, lured by the smell of honey that still lingered within. Near by a pile of poles half hidden in decayed straw betrayed some symptoms of having once been intended for a stable. A little farther on we came to the "ranche house." It was of the regulation pattern of the granger's house of that time—a mere shell of rough lumber mounted upon stilts, full in the sun, with its only window on the side from which in summer the breeze is certain never to come. Under a huge live-oak behind the house hung a box with door and back of wire screen, through which was dimly visible a long strip of desiccated bacon-rind with the butt-ends of departed slices standing along its inner surface, yellow and gray with time—a melancholy stub-book of past prosperity. All around the house were fragments of honey boxes, masses of dead bees and moth cocoons, broken glass, empty tin cans, rabbit-skins, and empty tobacco-sacks, while the outside of the house was adorned with nails full hung with an assortment of almost everything from a plow-clevis to a weather-beaten wild-cat skin.

A lank dog drew himself with considerable effort from under the house at our approach, gave a perfunctory bark, and hastily retreated to the shade he had unwisely left. As we rounded the corner of the house the sound of dragging feet came from within, then a stream of tobacco-juice cleared the soap-box that served for a door-stoop, and in another second a bushy head, ragged whiskers, and frowsy mustache came slowly into view around the door-post.

"Morning," drawled the owner of the head, propping himself with care against the door-post, and smiling as in my friend he recognized an old acquaintance.

"Come in," he added, as he shuffled himself inside, hooked one foot within one of the legs of a three-legged stool and gave it a lazy jerk into the middle of the floor, while with the other foot he kicked an empty nail-keg toward my companion.

"Take a seat," he continued, as, with a minimum of exertion that he had evidently studied out with long practice, he half slid and half tumbled upon a rough cot in one corner.

The solar heat of the autumn day upon the thin roof was increased by a fire in an open fireplace, where a flap-jack suitable for a cannon-wad was sputtering in a frying-pan.

"We'll have some dinner directly," said the owner of the frying-pan with a dubious glance at the half of a rabbit that lay on the table awaiting its turn in the frying-pan.

"Can't stop, thank you," said my companion, who had taken a hasty review of the larder. "How are the bees doing?"

"Fine! I ain't lost over two thirds of mine. Some of my neighbors have lost about all theirs. Last winter the rain was too light and the feed short, and they robbed their bees too close. I didn't have to rob mine. They were so hungry they robbed each other and saved me the trouble," said the granger.

"You raise good fruit here, I suppose?" I remarked quite innocently.

"The blue-jays and linnets think so. I never had a chance to sample any of it myself."

"That land along the creek looks like good garden-land," said my friend; "you raise good vegetables there, of course."

"I've laid down lots of them. I never raised any yet."

"But you certainly raise your own potatoes?"

"No; the squirrels raise them for me."

"And don't you have any garden at all?"

"Had one, one year, but the chickens got away with it."

"I don't see any chickens around here now."

"Of course not. The wild-cats got away with them by the time they had finished the garden."

"Did you ever try the raisin-grape here?"

"Planted some once, but the rabbits eat off the buds as fast as they came out."

"Well, you get even on the rabbits, don't you?" said my friend with a wink at me that showed that he was drawing out the man for amusement.

"The rabbits don't owe me anything," replied the man. "I would have been busted long ago without them. But they are getting so scarce now, that I have to go three or four hundred yards from the house to get one. It's a cold day when I have to split a rabbit to make two meals out of. The outlook for grub is getting really serious," he added with an anxious glance at the half of a rabbit.

"And didn't any of the vines grow at all?" asked my friend.

"Well, a few did, but the deer closed them out in the fall."

"And can't you get even on the deer? That's the way I do."

"Too much resemblance to work, tramping over these hills."

"But wine-grapes ought to do well, and deer don't bother them much."

"Quails!" replied the man with a sigh.

"I should think this would make a good hog-ranche," continued my friend.

"Splendid. I've got several dozen; they don't require any care here at all; I haven't had to look after mine for three years. But I know they are safe; a grizzly bear couldn't catch them in the chapparal, and no man would ever try it."

"Why didn't you fence them in?" I asked.

"What! and buy feed for 'em? Stranger, if it's a fair question, may I inquire where you were raised?"

"You ought to raise good corn on that land over there," said my friend.

"See those crows sitting in the sycamores? Tried it once. They are waiting for me to try it again. I'm waiting for them to die of disappointment."

"Why don't you try alfalfa? Crows don't pull that up."

"Had just that brilliant idea myself once. It only cost me a hundred dollars, though; that's the cheapest experience I've had here."

"Why, what was the matter?"

"Gophers," sighed the man.

"Have you tried grain?"

"Did you ever strike a darned fool here yet that didn't? I put in forty acres once. The header-man, threshing-machine-man and the warehouse-man in town all did well on it."

"And how did you come out?"

"Only lost some three hundred dollars."

"Why, that wasn't so bad," I remarked.

"O no; it might have been a heap worse; I got out cheap. One of my neighbors lost his ranche by his crop."

"I suppose then that hay or something you could harvest with your own work would be better," said I, as soon as I had discovered the point of the last answer.

"That's exactly what I thought; so I sowed it with barley for hay the next year. There was hardly any rain, and I had to pull it up by the roots to get any hay."

"Why didn't you let your horse harvest it himself?" said my friend, seeing that I was floored by the last answer.

"Before it got big enough I had to give him away to keep from buying feed for him. The sheepmen used up all the grass within ten miles."

"How long have you been here?"

"Something like six thousand."

"I asked how long you had been here."

"Well, I tell you some six thousand. Don't you know yet how to measure time in this country?"

"O yes, I take. But what have you done with it all?"

"Well, there's nearly five hundred dollars of it in that orchard," said the rancher, pointing to a few rows of dead sticks in various stages of decay.

"What is the matter with them?"

"Cattle broke them all down rubbing against them. You may notice that good rubbing posts are scarce in this country."

"Why didn't you fence them in?"

"Did, but a fire came up the canyon one day and took it."

"Your oranges don't seem very thrifty," continued my friend, pointing to some sorrowful-looking trees, of which one half were brown and the rest a yellowish green.

"I let them all go; it's too much trouble to manage an irritating ditch."

"A what?" I asked.

"He means an irrigating ditch," suggested my companion.

"No, I mean exactly what I said," said the granger—"an irritating ditch—the irritatingest thing on earth. When you get ready to use it you find that a gopher has made a hole in the dam and let out all the water. You get the hole fixed and the dam filled again, and then you find a dozen gopher holes in the ditch. Each one of them will let out all the water, and you can't find the worst ones until you have turned in the water. Then by the time you get the ditch fixed another gopher has made a hole in the dam, and when you get that stopped there are some more gopher holes in the ditch. By the time you have it fixed it's dinner-time, and by the time you are done smoking and get rested and ready for work it's so near night that you think it better to wait till next day. If the gophers haven't got away again with it by that time you are in luck, and even if they haven't, the sides of the ditch are so dry that half the water is lost by seepage and evaporation, and by the time you have coaxed it around a dozen trees you wish you had never been born, especially when you reflect that you have got to go over the whole programme again in about three days more or the ground will bake as hard as a petrified brick."

"Then what do you live on, if you don't raise anything?" asked my friend.

"Credit. Haven't you been here long enough to learn that trick?"

"I exhausted mine some time ago."

"What are you doing then?" asked the granger with more interest than he had yet shown.

"Poising."

"Poising? What's that?"

"Did you never see a hawk poising—hanging still in the air watching for something to drop on? That's my business at present."

"Well, as long as you can keep afloat on wind I would advise you not to drop on anything in this country."

"Why don't you get a wife? A man needs a helpmeet for success on a farm as well here as anywhere else."

"I don't need any help in getting clear of grub, and that is the only thing I will make a success of in this country. My family is already too big for this ranche."

"I suppose you might be induced to sell?"

"Well—yes—I—might. I have made enough out of it, and would be willing to let some one else have a show. There is nothing small about me."

"And then what would you do?"

"Go to work for somebody that had a ranche. In two years I would own it."

"Yes, and he would turn around and work for you and get it back in another two years."

"Not much. I would be too smart to run another ranche in this country. I would unload it on some tender-foot."

"Then you would return to the East, I suppose," I remarked.

"Not a bit of it," replied the granger with an air of intense disgust. I like Southern California too well for my own good. She is a tricky damsel, first-rate to flirt with, but of no account as a business partner. But I love her in spite of her tricks, and not even the archangel's trump can ever raise my bones from her soil."

Emerging from the canyon in which lay the "ranche" of the bachelor granger, our way lay for miles over a dreary stretch of gray sand, half covered with a thin and sorry-looking gray brush about knee-high. Scarcely a lobe even or cactus relieved the monotonous, gray of the sand and brush. Scarcely a sign of life relieved the hot glare of the vast expanse of desert save an occasional hare sitting in the exasperating shade of some little low bush just thick enough to stop all the breeze and just thin enough to let through the last beam of the midday sun. Each hare looked weary and mad, yet wore withal a look of mild resignation akin to that of the granger we had just left. Nowhere within sight was there for him any means of support, and yet it was evident that, like the granger, he did not wish to leave the country. It was from these two fixtures that I had my first conception of living on climate.

Deeply scarred at intervals with a ragged gash made by some rush of water from the mountains and at other intervals covered with a great wash of boulders, cobble-stones and coarse sand from the same source, miles of this wretched-looking stuff stretched away toward the bottom of the valley, where a few distant lines of green showed the possibility of some settlement. The man who for an instant would have dreamed of any one living on this desert would have been deemed insane, and at that time probably would have been so. I could have bought thousands of acres of it for a song, but neither my companion nor I would have paid the land-office fees to preëmpt the whole of it. And the oldest residents of the country were the most pronounced of all in their opinion that it was utterly worthless for any purpose and for all time.

Many a reader will take most of the above for a very weak attempt to be funny. But it is written in sober earnest, and does not describe one half of the difficulties that then beset every man who departed from raising live-stock and tried to coax a dollar or even worry a living out of the soil; except in a few places around Los Angeles, where some money was made by sending a few oranges to the limited market of San Francisco. So universal were the troubles of the common farmer and fruit-grower, that most of them were chronic grumblers, taking a positive satisfaction in relating their experience. Everywhere one could hear people tell a more harrowing tale than the one above; and they would tell it with genuine gusto, and apparently with more satisfaction before a stranger than when alone. Many an hour's amusement the writer has had from sea-coast to mountain-top, drawing out the unfortunates by questions which he soon learned to frame. Yet with all their troubles they were all like the bachelor granger and the hare. They were all mad and sad, but none of them wanted to leave the country. Although nearly every place in the land was for sale, it was not to get money with which to leave the country, but to repeat the same folly somewhere on another place that seemed to have better conditions.

As long as production was subject to so many drawbacks there was no prospect of a boom, and nobody thought of any. But in the next ten years the land underwent a change which was probably the most rapid and radical that the world has ever seen.

CHAPTER II.

THE CHANGES OF TEN YEARS.

In the winter of 1885 I chanced again to visit the place of the bachelor granger. But for the towering mountains that looked solemnly down upon it with their timbered heads and sides all robed in white, I should hardly have recognized the place. It had long been in other hands, and its first owner had gone back into the hills to repeat on a new farm the folly that had cost him this one.

On one side of the little valley, upon a broad knoll, once crowned with cactus and piles of granite that formed a perfect citadel for the rabbits and squirrels that had ravaged the garden of the former owner, stood now a large and handsome house, surrounded with verdure of every shade, upon which were embroidered all the colors of the rainbow. Hedges of lime, cypress, and pomegranate enclosed the place, and India-rubber, camphor, umbrella, and other tropical trees shaded the walks.

Encircled by hedges of geranium aglow with scarlet light lay smooth little lawns of varied grasses, with stars and circles and diamond-shaped centerpieces of heliotrope, pansy, calla, fuchsia, and what not, all of great size, and bright and fresh as if born of last night's dew. The rocks that once looked so formidable had all been blasted away except a few left here and there in fantastic piles, from the centers of which fountains played over shining green tangles of curious vines and ferns. The porches and lower story of the house were nearly lost in a profusion of nasturtiums, roses, honeysuckles, and geraniums, that were climbing over everything upon which they could get a foothold, and pouring a flood of color over the whole.

From this knoll the land at first descended toward the hill in a gentle slope, and then rose in long lines of orange, lemon, and olive trees, apricots, prunes, peaches, nectarines, and pears, and grape-vines of some thirty varieties. Ten years before, this hillside seemed too steep to run even a plow upon. But fully two thirds of its slope seemed to have disappeared with cultivation. Then the soil seemed thin, hard, and worthless as a burnt brick, and bearing no grass or other vegetation but a thin gray brush, that wore a sad and weary air as if worsted in the struggle for existence. Its former owner never imagined that it would produce even a white bean, and had hesitated long about preëmpting the place because the government lines ran in such a way that, in order to get the bottom-land along the creek that he wanted, he had to include this in his entry and pay a dollar and a quarter an acre for it. Though rich as the best of prairie, the bottom land which he then deemed the only thing of value was now the least valuable part of the whole, and was devoted entirely to the raising of corn and hay, and to pasture; while on the miserable-looking hillside twenty acres of oranges but five years old from the nursery were paying an income of ten per cent a year on the total cost of the place and all its improvements. Apricots, peaches, and nectarines not as old were already netting seventy-five dollars an acre, forty acres of Muscat grapes were turning off nearly a ton of raisins to the acre, and next year the olives would repay the entire cost of their planting and care, and yield a steady income thereafter.

The difficulties to which the former owner succumbed were all mastered. A well-built hen-house fastened at night protected a hundred chickens. A light fence of lath at the bottom of the hedges kept out all the rabbits. The owner's boy with his little 22-caliber rifle had the bluejays and other mischievous birds almost exterminated, and if he had not, the quantity of fruit in season was so great that the few birds there were could make no impression upon it. With a shotgun the same boy kept the quails out of the vineyard in grape time, and had plenty of fun and all the quails the house could use as well. The destructive ground-squirrels had all disappeared by being treated to poisoned wheat at the right time of the year, and in similar ways all other pests were disposed of completely. And the little stream of water that our old friend had found such a nuisance was the source of all this wealth. It had been taken out much higher up the stream than before, increased by tunneling to three times its former flow, brought down in a cement pipe to a point on the hill about a hundred feet higher than the old owner had ever thought of using it, and part of it was piped to the house under a pressure that threw it over the top of the chimney. Instead of pouring on more water to prevent the baking of the ground, cultivation, which the granger had never thought of, was now used. By this the ground was kept mellow and moist so long that it was now necessary to irrigate but four or five times a year instead of twice a week, and for the grapes and deciduous fruits two or three times, according to the character of the season, was now sufficient.

Even more striking was the change that had come over the broad slope of gray sand that ten years before had excited my sympathies for the poor hare that fate had condemned to live on it. Near its outer edge I found what seemed the same old hare, sitting in the same old aggravating shade of the same old emaciated bush. But he now looked happy and fat—so much so that I felt called upon to gather him in. Half a mile beyond where he sat lay a long stretch of bright green, above which rose the gables and cupolas of hundreds of houses, mingled with the spires of churches and the bell-towers of imposing school-houses. Up to the very edge of it the land lay sad and gray as ever, then suddenly changed into a maze of green as I crossed a cement-lined ditch in which sparkling water from the mountains was winding its eddying way.

Down a long avenue lined with eucalyptus and pepper trees and feathery palms I rode, with hedges of cypress and arbor vitæ on either side, enclosing places where handsome houses of every style of architecture stood embowered in brilliant shrubbery. The linnet was warbling from the apricot-tree, and from the orange the mocking-bird was pouring out his joy over the coming of the rains; the lark in the almond was tuning up his winter harp, and the long-silent thrush was discovering that the time to sing had come again. On smoothly shaven lawns, starred with groups of date-palm, banana, and pampas-plumes, children were rolling and tumbling; on the porches young girls in summer dress were reading bare-headed in hammocks under arcades of roses and geraniums; and just behind them all, apparently within rifle-shot, rose two miles into the sky a great mountain clad from crown to base in glittering snow.

Nowhere was there a fence to be seen. The whole was one continuous garden and orchard of five, ten, and twenty acre tracts separated only by hedges of pomegranate, guava, lime, or cypress, and often only by rose or geranium. Groves of lemon, orange, and other fruit trees and vineyards were on every hand, and the only thing bearing the slightest resemblance to common farming was an occasional

Jersey cow tethered on half an acre or so of brightly green alfalfa.

Vainly I looked for the gray sand that ten years before appeared so unutterably barren, and on the outside of the ditch still seemed the same. In the dooryards it was all hidden by the sheets of spangled green that sprung beneath the play of revolving fountains. In the orchards and vineyards it had changed under the plow to a chocolate-colored loam, in which a few specks of quartz and feldspar shining here and there were all that remained of the sandy appearance. The cobble-stones and bowlders had been removed or heaped into fantastic rock-piles covered with flowers, or broken into material for walks or concrete for the ditches. New houses were rising, and new orchards and vineyards were stretching out far beyond the limits of the settlement; and this sorry looking stuff of a few years ago was now selling rapidly to immediate settlers for two hundred dollars an acre.

Sharp as was this contrast between the old and the new, it was scarcely more so than the contrast between these once barren uplands and the lowlands, once deemed the only lands of any possible value. A few miles away, at the foot of this long slope of coarse wash from the great mountains, lay the bottom of the valley—a broad sweep of fine, deep alluvium, fertile as any land under the sun. But the settlement upon it bore a painful resemblance to that of ten years before, with many suspicious symptoms of possible retrogression. There were the same broad fields of deep, rich soil; the same long expanses of moist land, always damp enough to raise stupendous crops without irrigation. Acre for acre, this land would raise in a series of years heavier crops of corn, grass, alfalfa, beets, pumpkins, sweet potatoes, and similar stuff than any lands in the Eastern States. Yet it was evidently not sought by the new settlers, and no new houses were rising upon it. What farms there were upon it were almost as scattered, as old-fashioned and cheerless as in the past. Almost the whole of it was devoted to corn, alfalfa, and pasture, with a few of the owners still clinging to their old orchards and vineyards, though for most fruits and vines time had proved them of little value as compared with those on the uplands.

A glance at the people showed them radically different from those on the upland. They were mostly of the old-time lazy, dawdling set, striving only to make a careless living with the least amount of work, and caring little for the beauty of their surroundings. Occasionally a grove of English walnuts on land not too wet was yielding heavy profits, and some other trees and vines were doing very well; but on the greater part of the land it was common farming of the most common kind. Some of the settlers sneered at the people on the upland as a lot of fools who would soon get tired of working poor land and would some day know good land when they saw it; but the majority were quite willing to sell and follow the example of the " fools" on the higher slopes.

Even more striking was the change in the quality of the fruit the country was now producing and in the way it was put up for market. In 1875 nothing worthy of the name orange could be seen in California. Thick-skinned, sour, pithy, and dry, it was an insult to the noblest of fruit to call the California product by that name. Though a few in San Francisco bought them because at the time of the year when they are ripe they could get none elsewhere, they were not fit to eat, or even to look at. The lemons, great overgrown things, with skin half an inch thick over a dry and spongy interior, were more worthy of pity than contempt. In the winter of 1884-5 the oranges and lemons of Southern California, in competition with those of almost the whole world, swept away all the premiums at the New Orleans Exposition, and the oranges were then selling on the Eastern market in a way that showed that the premiums were based upon true merit. Placing the orchards on the high land, discarding the old methods of irrigation, and using less water and more plow, caused almost the whole of the change.

In 1880 a California raisin was deservedly a laughing-stock in the few markets where the packer had the impudence to offer them. By 1885 people had discovered that labeling dried grapes "raisins" did not make them so, and that the trick of filling the middle of the box with the poorest ones was neither funny nor profitable. I hesitate to record such an astonishing truth, but it is also a fact that in those five short years they also discovered that the trick was not original. Every packer had acted as if he had worked it out as a bran-new conception. In five short years he found that others had thought of the same thing. Having learned that care in curing and honesty in packing were as essential as the soil or the sunshine that made the grape what it is, people were in 1885 turning out a raisin which foretold the easy victory they have since won in every market in which their raisins have been introduced.

Similar improvement had been made in almost every other branch of cultivation of the soil. Peaches, prunes, apricots, pears, nectarines, and other fruits that hitherto had gone to waste were now being canned and dried, and were all paying an income to the acre that no Eastern farmer ever dreams of. Common farming, too, where carried on with one half the industry, economy, and business prudence necessary in the rest of the world, would now insure a better living, with fewer discomforts, than farming anywhere else. Though it could not approach fruit-growing as a source of profit or as an easy and pleasant out-of-door occupation for those having no love for heavy work, it had advanced enough to prove conclusively that Southern California was by no means dependent upon fruit-growing, and that the man who could not buy good fruit land could make a prosperous home in thousands of places where ten years before not even the rabbits could have saved him.

Nearly all of this change had been wrought by a class of emigrants that scarcely any other section in the world has ever seen. Nearly all of them were people of means—many of them quite wealthy—all seeking a change of climate. Though some came for their own health, or the health of some member of their family, the majority were in no sense invalids. They were simply weary of bad weather of every description, and able to spend the rest of life in a place where they would be free from it. Such people were determined to have pleasant homes with some beauty around them, whether it were profitable or not. If at the same time a place could be made profitable as well as handsome, so much the better. Separately, and on isolated tracts, many had been working out the problem of raising the finest fruits merely for pleasure, and with no expectation that it would repay the outlay. Others, as at Riverside, were working on the problem in concert, and with a firm conviction that it would some day repay them, but still determined to experiment whether it ever were profitable or not. Few undertakings could seem more hopeless than the raising of anything on the dry slope, hard and bare as the floor of a brick-yard, where Riverside now glows in beauty. Yet its founders were firm in their faith. They let the laughers laugh, and devoted themselves to the water-ditch and the cultivator. Before the owners of the rich bottom-lands had finished their smile three thousand acres of this wretched-looking stuff were bringing the owners more money to the acre than any other equal area in the United States.

By the year 1885 it was plain that this turning over to cattle and swine of the fertile meadows, green all summer with mallow and clover and silvery grass, and the bottom-lands where the cottonwood, sycamore, and willow intertwined with great wild grapevines, the whole casting a dense shade over the richest soil in America, was no mere whim of the passing hour. There was no malaria there, the soil was always damp and needed little or no irrigation, and enormous crops were a certainty. Yet the land would not bring the same price it had brought in many places years before; while the barren-looking stuff a few hundred feet above it, which in its natural state needed fifty acres to keep a sheep in some seasons, was now selling readily at five or six times what the other had ever sold for.

This great difference was due—

First, to the discovery that, though some lands were much richer than others, all land that could be plowed at all, no matter what its appearance, its condition, or its subsoil, was good enough if properly irrigated.

Second, the discovery that the difference in the temperature of winter nights on the lowlands and on the uplands was a steady difference to the owner of many dollars to the acre.

Third, to the fact that nearly all kinds of valuable trees on the bottom-lands were sooner or later injured, and often killed, by the roots going into standing water below the surface; and as this water was subject to change of level with the varying amount of rainfall in different winters, it was next to impossible to know where to put a tree on the bottom-land so that the water-level could not rise upon its roots.

What wonder, then, that the news of all these changes went abroad?—that people who came to look were enraptured, as people had always been, with the soft climate, and now were pleased with the idea of enjoying it, and at the same time making profit out of it by the easiest of all out-of-door work? Was it not now evident that these irrigated lands were going to support the largest population to the acre of any lands in the United States? Was it not plain that the once despised "cow counties" which the northern part of the State had long sneered at were fast becoming the most valuable part of the State for the area? No one who would take the trouble to look around and examine the shipping receipts and account books of the fruit-buyers, who were already established in business and were buying for cash the fruit upon the vines and trees and picking and packing it themselves, and were bidding against one another for anything and everything, could any longer doubt it. The discoveries of the few years preceding had expanded by many hundred fold the productive area of the country, and so increased the power of each acre that the future was now beyond question.

CHAPTER III.

THE BEGINNING OF THE BOOM.

So constantly accumulating on every side were the proofs of the wonderful results of the skillful management of an irrigating stream on the warm uplands of the southern counties under a sun where so many things grow the whole year through, that a steady increase in travel was the result. Before the spring of 1885 nearly all visitors came only in winter. Like birds of passage, the whole flock took wing as soon as the almanac announced that spring had come, leaving only a few who concluded to settle. Almost universal was the impression that the heat of the summer must be intolerable. "If the winter is so fine, what must the summer be?" was a very natural question for the many who do not know that the great Gulf Stream of this coast is from a polar gulf instead of from a tropical gulf, as on the Atlantic. Instead of going to the records of the United States Signal Service, which had been kept here for many years, they sought the answer in their own imaginations. Such records are only used by cranks and bookworms. Your "practical man," who knows enough to make some money in this world, evolves all such information from his inner consciousness. The richer he is the less use he has for any such theoretical nonsense as records. With a week's observation he can tell you every peculiarity of the climate without bothering with any records. As he is rich, most people believe that he knows all about it, and thus the knowledge of the climate of the country is spread through the East. Consequently the travel had been like that into Florida—a few weeks' run of midwinter tourists, of whom a small percentage remained to settle.

But, to the surprise of all, the travel in the spring of 1885, instead of falling off, remained about the same as in the winter, and continued so all summer. It had long been noticed that though the majority of the settlers were people who had been captured by the fine weather of the winter, a much larger proportion had always been ensnared by the summer. Thousands had spent a winter here and gone away, never to return. But of the hundreds who dallied with the long, bright summer, with its dry air, cool nights, and unfailing sea-breeze, few ever went away to stay long.

This difference was now more striking than ever, and before summer was half over the rate of settlement was much more rapid than formerly, and prices were already rising a little. New houses were dotting the landscapes far and near; new settlements like Redlands were springing here and there; Los Angeles, Pasadena, and San Bernardino were growing rapidly; on the north Santa Barbara and San Buenaventura were beginning to feel the effect; and even San Diego began to rub its eyes after the long sleep that followed the collapse of the Texas Pacific Railroad some twelve years back.

The winter of 1885–6 came on, and travel increased as never before and began some six weeks earlier than usual. The retired banker who had long forgotten his brother, who for years had been struggling with ill-health and the combined difficulties that beset all the earlier settlers of this country, and whose appeals for a small loan had been always met with the answer "Money is very tight just now," suddenly remembered him when he heard he was now making some money, and came out to pay him a visit instead of paying board at a hotel in Florida. The rich merchant who had heretofore gone to Florida, hearing that wealthy people were now going to California, concluded that he would try it. The wealthy broker, whose curiosity is always excited by the report that somebody is making some money somewhere, came also to examine the situation. Professional tourists, hearing that there were now some good hotels in California and good eating-houses along the way, and Pullman cars to ride in, concluded to add Southern California to their stock of subjects to talk about. People who had been here before and were pleased with everything but the prospects of making anything out of the soil, hearing now of its great advance, came back to see if there were sufficient inducement to stay. Along with these came invalids and other climate-seekers, and people whose relatives here had been advising them to come out, and farmers by the hundred, tired of vibrating for seven months in the year between the fireplace and the wood-pile, dodging cyclones and taking quinine. And with these came schemers and promoters of all kinds, with a little money which they were anxious to increase at the expense of some one else and without risking any of their own; and capitalists of high and low degree, who had heard that the country was prosperous, for prosperity makes friends for a country as well as for persons.

The winter of 1885-6 was well adapted to capture any one, for the rains had come early and by the middle of January the whole land was a rolling sheet of green. He who stood on any of the higher hills around Los Angeles with a good glass could see an area of country immediately around the city that when worked to its full capacity under the improved methods of the time would make almost a State in itself. Below him, surrounded by a wealth of green reaching away from the center in long lines of ten, twenty, and forty acre tracts, lay a rapidly growing city of some twenty thousand people, scattered amid groves of oranges in which the golden gleam of the ripening fruit and the snowy bloom of the crop to come contrasted brightly with the dark sheen of the evergreen leaves. Miles away into the southeast until lost in the hazy green of the great San Joaquin rancho reached a vast plain sloping gently up to the foot of the Santa Ana mountains, and as gently down on the south to the edge of the great shining ocean. From there to where the verdant carpet of the land curled up into the highlands above San Pedro and on the west rolled away to where Santa Monica slept beside the sea, villages, hamlets, and farms dotted the land on every side. Dark groves of oranges, deep-green fields of alfalfa, orchards of English walnut, apricot, and other deciduous fruits, and mile upon mile of vineyard spread out before him on every hand; miles of dark earth freshly upturned where the great gang-plows were putting in grain, and miles of green beside them where the grain already sown was brightening over the land. Above the dense shade of the eucalyptus, cypress, and pepper trees that hid the vineyards and orchards in their midst, the spires and roofs of Anaheim, Santa Ana, Orange, Tustin, and others of the larger settlements were dimly visible. Larger farms bearing every sign of high prosperity filled the intervals between these settlements, except where some great rancho, still undivided, spread out its leagues of land, on which large herds of cattle and horses were nibbling the springing grass. Miles away the eye could trace the shining threads of the water-ditches that caused most of this wealth, and by the long lines of timber could follow the courses of the rivers, and through the openings in the trees could see the sparkle of their waters.

On the northwest to where the plains of Santa Monica sloped into the Cahuenga hills one saw the same alternation of immense ranchos, orchards and vineyards, broad pastures dotted with horses and cattle, and thousand-acre fields darkly brown with earth fresh from the plow. If he turned his glass over the Cahuenga hills, the valley of San Fernando shone brightly green with tens of thousands of acres of wheat and barley. If he turned it easterly into the great valley of San Gabriel, long wavy swells of slope and vast reaches of plain, the whole looking as if smoothly shaven and powdered with emerald dust, stretched leagues away to where the snowy heads of San Antonio, San Jacinto, and Greyback looked down from two miles of majesty upon the fertile valley of San Bernardino. And here in San Gabriel, too, were long lines of shade-trees, and sparkling watercourses and artesian wells, and large groves of orange and lemon that rivaled the dark green of the groves of live-oaks still standing on some of the larger ranchos.

Everywhere in the wide circle around the visitor, wreathed in a blaze of flowers, rose houses such as he had never before seen in any farming country, and new places were brightening on almost every plain and slope and hill where but lately all was open cattle-range. Such a sight was a novelty to any one from the East. Nowhere else in the world had such a class of settlers been seen. Emigrants coming in palace-cars instead of "prairie schooners," and building fine houses instead of log shanties, and planting flowers and lawn-grass before they planted potatoes or corn, were a grand surprise. And yet one sweep of the glass around the circle showed him that the people who were doing it were coming faster than ever. And it was plain that they had come to stay. The man of means who at this time could spend an hour on any hill from which a good view of Los Angeles County could be had without calling on a real-estate agent before sundown was the exception, and not the rule.

But perhaps the stranger concluded to look about a little more, and went down to San Diego. There he saw from the heights above the town the whole surroundings of the bay with a single sweep of the eye. From the long promontory of Point Loma, which miles away on the west forms one barrier of the harbor, to the table-lands of

Tia Juana fifteen miles in the southeast, from the water's edge to the highest point of the slope, the whole lay undulating in a hundred shades of green under the soft sunlight that streamed from the clear sky. From every direction in the city below him came the sound of the saw and the hammer; and at National City, the terminus of the Santa Fé Railroad, four miles up the bay, new houses not yet ready for the paint were glimmering in all the freshness of new lumber. Miles away on either hand shone the bright water of the bay, unbroken save by the dark hulls of the shipping or the splash of the fish-hawk and pelican. Coronado Beach, the outer guard of the harbor, had then no settlers except the coyote, the hare, and the quail; but its green chapparal and thousands of springing flowers and its happy location on the bay plainly foretold its future. Beyond it lay the great Ocean of Peace, its shimmering face smooth as the bay within, except where a few lines of lazy foam curling up on the shore were trying to keep up the appearance of an ocean. Miles away on its unruffled plain rose the rugged outlines of the Coronado Islands, changing into fantastic forms under the mirage formed by the mirror of the sea. In the south in rank upon rank rose the mountains of Mexico, hazily blue with distance; and on the east, chain upon chain of pine-fringed ridges ran away into the north until they curled swiftly up into great snowy peaks, like white clouds floating in the far-off blue. But what pleased the eye of the stranger more than all else were the miles and miles of slope that in every direction rolled from the highlands toward the bay with just the right descent for perfect drainage, yet wide enough and smooth enough for a vast city. His fancy readily covered the bay with wharves, and on the horizon's utmost verge it saw the white wings of commerce looming up from the Occident, laden with the wealth of China, Japan, and Australia, and all steered by the pilot of especial destiny for what the United States charts showed was one of the best harbors in the world.

The probabilities were very strong that before another sun lit up the scene this man also called upon a real-estate agent.

But perhaps the stranger was unusually wise, and concluded to look still farther, and hied him away to the county of San Bernardino.

Here he found nearly half a million acres of rich land lying in a body beneath an almost tropical sun, and surrounded by lofty mountains, upon whose tops glittered eternal snow scarcely fifteen miles from where the orange, lemon, and banana were growing. Down the dark ravines from the snow-banks above came sparkling streams winding out on the slopes and table-lands, in ditches and flumes, and pipes of cement or iron, while miles of new aqueduct were building in every direction. New orchards were planting on every hand, and thousands of acres of vineyard and green fields of alfalfa were stretching across the valley and reaching far out upon the lately bare and sun-baked plains. He found scores of men making not only a living but a good profit besides out of only ten acres, forcing the land by control of the water to a productive power of which he had never imagined any soil capable. He found people cutting grain, then irrigating the land and planting corn which they would harvest in August, then planting potatoes which they were to dig in November, and have the ground again green with another crop of grain by Christmas. He found them raising berries and vegetables and corn and even alfalfa in the young orchards between the rows of trees, the advantages of proper irrigation being so great that one could in this way use the intermediate ground while waiting for the trees to mature. In the country new houses were rising on every slope, and the city of San Bernardino was growing, with a growth clearly compelled by that of the surrounding country, and solidly safe for an investor. Its people did no boasting of climate, or scenery, or future commercial advantages. They pointed with pride only to the miles of rich soil around their doors, to the shining lines of the water-ditches, and to the artesian wells that glittered around them over thousands of acres, and even in the city were so numerous that almost every poor man could at small cost have his own system of water-works.

The man who for a single day could look over such scenes without at least having some curiosity about prices was rare.

But possibly all this seemed to him too new. It was only within a very short time that the making of a profit or even a living on ten acres had been a success, and it was not yet certain that it could be done everywhere. Nor was it certain that fruit, however good, would always command such prices as at present, he thought.

"Something a little more solid and old-fashioned would suit me better," he perhaps said to himself, and then went to see the counties of Ventura and Santa Barbara.

If he went into them at the opening of spring he was quite sure to feel a curiosity about prices. Through the waving grain of the valley of San Fernando he rode, and over a low range of mountains he descended into the valley of the Santa Clara River. All the colors of the rainbow were racing in mad confusion over the carpet of green that rolled over hill and dale. Far up the mountain sides and even amid the silvery foxtail grass that shone so softly bright beneath the time-bowed live-oaks, purple and gold and crimson and blue were struggling for the mastery. The river was whirling along to the sea through banks clad in long grass, wild-rose, and sweetbrier, with tangles of wild-grape overshadowed by willow, cottonwood, and sycamore, and its mica sands sparkling like flakes of gold as they rolled over in its swift waters. The dazzle of flowers grew brighter as the valley became wider in its descent to the coast, and the stranger was well prepared to be captured even before he reached the well-settled portion. Farm after farm soon opened before him, with fields of deep alfalfa along the river bottom, broad fields of grain on the low slopes that led away from it, and great fields of beans, rivaling in size even the fields of grain, which were themselves often larger than those of the prairie States. Cattle and horses sleek with fatness stood breast-deep in the pastures, or dozed away the noontide in groups beneath the live-oaks, while orchards and vineyards spread far away up the steeper slopes that led to the mountains. He saw few ten-acre tracts, but mainly large farms, and every place wore an air of old-time solidity. Even the houses that shone from the live-oak groves at the heads of the great washes a thousand feet or more above the valley, or still higher up on the shoulders of the lofty hills that inclosed the scene, wore the same air. Though it might take the owner half a day to go home, the fields of grain that waved along the hillsides, the vineyards and orchards that shone over acres of drift from the mountain, the long lines of bee-hives beside them, and the living stream that wound through lines of green alders down from the hills far above the house, enabled him when he did reach home to look down with serene contempt on the world below.

If the stranger ever wondered where Boston got its beans, he found out now, as the land fell away to the Pacific with the soil becoming richer and finer as it expanded into the broad plains of Santa Paula and Hueneme, green for miles with grain and springing corn and beans, and groves of blooming trees and budding vines. Prosperity smiled on every side, and the farmers were making more money to the acre than the ordinary Eastern farmer ever dreams of.

In Santa Barbara County the stranger found much the same kind of land, but sloping from a high mountain range to the ocean in long rolling waves, bearing upon its bosom hundreds of farms and orchards, with hundreds of houses looking down from their surrounding groves of moss-draped live-oaks upon the sea below and the dark green islands that rose from its smiling face.

If a cautious man, looking only for a productive farm in a safe country, all this pleased the stranger. But while some of the visitors flattered themselves that they were looking for such a place, they were really looking for a chance to double their investments, without waiting too long. To such, this part of the country seemed all too slow. The great groves of English walnuts were undoubtedly profitable, and there was no danger of drugging the market with the product. Equally certain seemed the orchards of olive, pear, prune, peach, and nectarine; while in the broad fields of grain and beans there seemed no danger at the prices then asked. The long slopes, too, where so many new houses were rising above the brilliant coloring of the greensward, were cheap enough. But along the radiant hills that exchanged smiles with the peaceful sea there was no rumble of any coming boom, in the lazy waves that were lapping the sunny sands no murmur of future speculation.

For such, Pasadena at this time offered the finest inducements outside of Los Angeles. The orchards, vineyards, and gardens of this fair place were not then suffering from neglect, as they were after the full force of the boom came upon it, but the whole lay radiant with prosperity. Mile upon mile down the great valley below them reached the residences of wealthy people who had been coming in for years; while the open ground between their places was covered with waving grain, wild-oats, and green pastureland, dotted with live-oaks and groups of cattle and horses. Beside long avenues lined with eucalyptus, cypress, and pepper trees, lay miles of orchard and vineyard, and long lines of new ones were creeping up the slopes to the very feet of the mountains upon whose tops the snow glistened for many a league.

Though far and near new houses were rising upon the slopes, the evidences of prosperity outside pleased many a visitor far less than the evidences of growth in the town itself. Its people, who but a year before had pointed with pride to their orchards and vineyards, were now absorbed in town-lot speculation, and their principal talk was of advances and margins, and the time within which money could be doubled. Orchards the year before laden with golden oranges were now white with stakes, and even the green alfalfa patches, with the little Jersey cow tethered upon them, and from which all the butter, milk, and eggs the family could use came from a single acre, were beginning to go the same way. From every point of the compass rang the sound of the hammer, and every day new people from the East were coming and buying and building. He who went there in one of those spring days, when all vegetation far and near was in the heyday of life, when the whole landscape was aglow with such color as he had never imagined could arise from an untilled garden, when the air was laden with fragrance and the evening sun was firing with rosy flame the white spires that towered a mile or more above him, was quite apt to think less about the productive power of the soil than about what some one else would pay for a small piece of it before another year.

But many a one withstood successfully all the temptations of the different sections, and felt a supreme indifference for all he saw. Many more saw nothing, made no attempt to see anything, and would not have known it if they had seen anything different from the country in which they had grown up. Many another was enraptured with the climate and scenery and wrote silly letters home about Paradises and "regular little Edens," but the strings of his purse relaxed not. For all such the auction which had just been introduced in Los Angeles by some professional boomers from Chicago and other points was admirably adapted.

CHAPTER IV.

THE SHEARING OF THE LAMBS.

THE Californians have been accused of shearing a drove of innocent lambs from the East. If true, this would have been one of the most interesting features of the times; for, as we shall see, the lambs afterward sheared the shearers in charming style. But the sad and homely truth is, that nearly all the innocents were wise and successful men, who insisted on being shorn. All through the boom the golden fleece was willingly shed, and the shearing was about in the manner following.

It was in the latter part of March, 1886, that, with step sedate and nose upturned in lofty contempt for everything in California except the climate, Mr. Brown, a wealthy merchant from New York, was pacing the pavement in Los Angeles anxiously awaiting the day when the almanac should inform him that it was warm enough in New York to return. Outside of New York he knew next to nothing, and could see nothing in California worthy of his notice except the climate, which he was gracious enough to pronounce "very fine." He found himself lingering instead of returning, and though resolving every day to start for home on the next day, there was something in the soft air and bright sunshine that still kept him.

A crash of brass and drums aroused him from his reverie of home as down the street came an omnibus filled with a brass band. Huge placards of cloth on the outside of the omnibus announced a grand auction sale of choice lots at "Excelsior Heights." Whereat the smoothly-shaven upper lip of the great merchant curled in wise disdain. But the curling process stopped suddenly short of completion, changed for an instant with the tension of deep meditation, and then to the indrawn tightness of resolution. What wrought the wondrous change deponent saith not, but he doth solemnly aver that at the bottom of the cloth placard in large red letters were the words:

"A free ride and a free lunch."

Another hour found Mr. Brown at "Excelsior Heights," nearly a mile out of the city. A brass band of some thirty pieces was storming the zenith, the performers resplendent in purple and gold and glittering helmets, with a drum-major, lost in swathings and bandings of scarlet and blue, twirling a gilded staff beneath a bale of crimson wool, while a caterer in dress-suit, with white necktie and diamond pin, was bustling to and fro preparing a sumptuous lunch.

Hundreds of people were already on the ground, and barouches and broughams, drawn by sleek horses in silver-plated harness driven by combinations of silk hats, white neckties, and dogskin gloves, were steadily unloading fat old bankers with their wives and daughters, retired merchants and stock-brokers, grain-dealers, liquor-dealers, lawyers and doctors, nearly all of whom, like Mr. Brown, had come out for a picnic at the expense of a stranger. None of them seemed to think there was anything mean in thus accepting the hospitality of the stranger when they had not the remotest idea of buying anything. And, strangely enough, the owner of the property did not think there was anything mean about it either; for he smiled and rubbed his hands as he looked over this portion of the crowd. These folks seemed to give him far more satisfaction than dozens of others who wore a business air, but little evidence of superfluous wealth.

The auctioneer, arrayed in costly garb, was an ex-minister of the Gospel who had been lured from the path of duty by the superior attractions of the rising real-estate market as compared with the size of his salary, and lacked the ripe experience of the owner of the property, an old hand from the East who had lately bought it on an option with a small payment down, and purposed making some money out of it before the time for the next payment came around.

"Picknickers, all of them. Out for a free ride and a free lunch," said the auctioneer to the owner with visible disgust. "They know no more of California than a mule knows about thoroughbred horses."

"Exactly what I want. They think they are doing something smart. You handle the boys right and I'll chance the results," said the owner.

The ex-parson was right. The greater part of the crowd consisted of mere tourists who for the first time in California had set foot outside the pavement, and knew just as much about the country as the great American tourist generally knows about any country. This tourist is a rare creature, especially in California. Most of the time he sits in the cars with his eyes lost in a novel or pack of cards or in the depths of some fair companion's eyes. While the train is running almost in the shadow of such mountains as he never saw before—mountains that tower above the country at their feet higher any other mountains in the United States, running, too, through a land where almost every herb and shrub and flower and tree and bird and animal is new to him, he rarely takes the trouble to glance out of the window. But let the train whistle for a station, and quickly he drops the novel or cards, and out goes his head from the window to stare at a house or hotel or something else that he could see just as well in ten thousand other cities in the United States. Of such material is the chap who writes up California in the Eastern papers, especially the one who is sent for that purpose because he is disinterested. He generally begins to scribble as soon as he reaches his hotel, takes a run around a few blocks in the center of town in the morning, and leaves on the evening train to decide with equal speed the fate of some other place.

But the owner of the property was also right. No Californian he, verdant enough to trust property at an auction to its naked merits. Right well he knew that real estate was very different from old furniture and old horses, and instead of selling for more than it is worth will sell for less, unless the judgment of the buyers is judiciously assisted. He was an old-time boomer, and had lately come to California because he fancied he heard the rumble of a coming boom. The natives knew nothing until such new-comers taught them, and even after they learned they rarely bettered the instruction of the new varieties of teachers that kept constantly coming with the latest Eastern ideas.

Mr. Brown soon discovered that there were many other wealthy people present. He never imagined that any of them were shrewd enough to do as he did, and have a picnic at the expense of some one else. He thought all the rest had come out purposely to buy, and that they seemed bent on buying something. Under the inspiring strains of the music and the congenial atmosphere of wealth his thoughts began to expand, his eyes for a moment actually wandered away from the bankers and roamed over the landscape. He saw for the first time the brilliant slopes that rolled away to the distant ocean, and the great islands of Santa

Catalina and San Clemente rising darkly green from the vast, shimmering plain. On the land between, the ripening grain and the slender wild-oats rippled beneath the sea-breeze in an undulating glow of silvery light, and where the alfileria and clover carpeted the slope they were starred with a thousand points of varied colors. The orchards that rose above the wavy land were now a mass of white and pink and the vineyards rivaled in brightness the rest of the green beside them.

As Mr. Brown gazed upon the scene he suddenly remembered that in his boyhood he had been in the country, and had seen some land that afterward had a city upon it. It suddenly occurred to him that some day this country might be worth something, that Los Angeles might possibly grow, and if it did, the tract now offered for sale might be worth something. Whereupon faintly dawned upon his mind the idea that handing out dry-goods over a New York counter was not the only way of making some money.

Like all property at that time on the market, " Excelsior Heights" was first-class, and will bring to-day, unimproved, ten times what was then paid for it, and that after two and a half years of steady decline. Still the owner was too old a real-estate operator to entrust land to its intrinsic merit alone at an auction on any kind of a market. He knew by long experience that the race of real-estate buyers are the silliest of sheep, and need leading even to their own good. And the auctioneer had been so often impressed with the sheep-like nature of man while trying to lead another kind of sheep to another kind of welfare, that he had no scruples about inveigling the crowd into what his conscience told him was really a fine bargain. So he had a dozen assistants distributed judiciously about the audience, none of whom were supposed to know one another or the auctioneer. Some were provided with gold coin to jingle on the table when they made their payments, while others who looked like business men had their check-books in their coat pockets. All appeared deeply verdant, and asked numerous questions about the country, its resources and prospects before the sale began.

After the band had nearly raised the roof off an immense live-oak under which they were stationed to protect the head of the drum-major from the sun, the auctioneer mounted the stand, announced the terms of sale, and pointing to a large cloth map on which a boy had located a lot with a long fishing-pole, said:

"Now, ladies and gentlemen, here is one of the finest lots in the whole tract, with the privilege of taking the next two, one of them the corner, at the same price. Give me a bid now, quick."

"A hundred dollars," called out a middle-aged man in gold spectacles, silk hat, and toothpick shoes.

All eyes were quickly turned upon him. But he stood their gaze without flinching. None suspected that he was an assistant. But he was, and had been in such haste to bid for fear the owner of some rival addition would bid only five or ten dollars so as to spoil the sale, that he forgot his instructions and bid fifty dollars less than he had been told.

"I am not selling you this map," said the auctioneer quickly, with withering tone. "It is a fifty-foot lot I am offering you. This map is only a reduced picture of it."

"One hundred and fifty," said, quietly and with the solemn dignity becoming a genuine buyer of wealth and standing, another man attired in trim broadcloth.

"One hundred and fifty only? Why, gentlemen,

this is positively ridiculous. These lots will bring a thousand dollars a piece in less than six months. Still, they have got to go. This sale is positively without reserve," said the auctioneer with an air of despondency. "One fifty, fifty, fifty; give us two hundred now, quick."

"I believe I will try that just for a flyer," said a thin-lipped man of some sixty years as he scratched a smoothly shaven chin with a gold eyeglass. "One fifty-five," he called out.

"Vy dot vos olt Squeems, de richest banker in Chicago. You bet he knows vot's goot," remarked to his neighbor a fat, red-faced man with pendulous cheeks acting as saddle-bags to a bulbous nose. "Hoondert and sixty," he called out after a moment's meditation.

"Hullo! That's old Katzenjammer of Milwaukee, one of the biggest brewers in the city," said Mr. Milton, a wealthy merchant from St. Paul, to his wife. "He is a mighty shrewd buyer, too. Just for fun, I will see how bad he wants that lot. It's good property anyhow, and I can't lose anything on it if it is knocked down to me. I don't know but what it would be well to invest a little here anyway." "One hundred and seventy," he called out to the auctioneer.

For a moment no one seemed inclined to bid higher, and the time for the assistants came around again. It had been understood that two hundred dollars was as high as it was safe to attempt to raise prices, and the price was now so near the top that it had to be raised very tenderly. So one of the assistants who looked like a banker shouted out, "A hundred and seventy-five."

"One seventy-five, five, five, five," rattled the auctioneer. "*Preeeeeee*posterous, gentlemen!" he cried. "Why, if this property was mine I would stop this slaughter right off. But the owner has advertised it without reserve, and he is one of those men who are fools enough to keep their word for the sake of being called honest. I am a pretty good judge of honesty myself, and there is no law human or divine that requires a man to throw away his property because he has been weak enough to assume that people will know a bargain when they see it."

"Pretty good property this, I declare," remarked Mr. Brown, looking around the landscape again after he had overheard the remark of the fat man from Milwaukee about the Chicago banker. But still he did not bid.

"One eighty," called out banker Squeems after remarking loud enough for several to hear: "There is no mistake about it. Los Angeles is going to be quite a city, and very soon too."

"Why don't you buy it?" asked the wife of a tristful-visaged, watery-eyed man who looked as if he had been weeping all night over the loss of a dime.

"Fiddlesticks! This country is good for nothing but climate," he replied.

"O, you think nothing is any good that's over a mile from Delmonico's," said his wife. "This is a nice country, and I want a lot here. Just hear the dear little birds sing. The flowers smell so sweet, too."

"Nonsense, my dear; those things don't make any money. I am a better judge of such things than you are," he said, as the lot was knocked off. The price had risen so near the critical point that none of the assistants dared to raise it any higher, and it went to the fat brewer for one hundred and ninety dollars. Yet even as he spoke in such contempt the watery eye of the man wandered over the land around, and his ears, hitherto deaf to all but the jingle of another dollar, were suddenly open to all its sounds.

It was one of those days so softly clear, so mildly bright, that characterize the greater part of March in this country; making the sharpest of contrasts with the leaden skies and howling blasts of the East. A medley of colors was blazing over hill and dale, acres of poppies with lustrous orange tints, acres of golden violets whose fragrance filled the breeze, everywhere the delicate pink of the alfileria and the tender blue of innumerable bell-flowers, with white and scarlet and purple rolling in gay confusion over the plains and up the feet of the hills to where the crimson of the wild pea, the lavender of the lilac, and the carmine of the wild gooseberry lit up the dark green of the chapparal. As he looked over this, while soft gurgling notes filled his ear from where the yellow breast of the lark shone amid the living green of the heteromeles, with the mocking-bird rolling out his soul from the orange-tree in the neighboring dooryard, and the twitter of the linnet coming fast and furious from the blooming almond, while the oriole joined the chorus from the live-oak close by, and the thrush chimed in from the adjoining chapparal, he was carried back to his early days when the sweet carol of the robin and the bubbling joy of the bobolink made the world seem brighter and fairer than it had ever seemed since.

"Well, my dear," he said at length, with the reserve becoming the importance of wealth that may possibly have to confess itself mistaken, "this may possibly amount to something some day, but I guess we had better see how things sell before investing."

But Mr. Brown was still obdurate. With the composure of independent wealth he saw a choice corner started at one hundred and sixty dollars, and gently raised a few dollars at a time by the "cappers" whenever there was any lagging in the bidding. At last the fat brewer and banker Squeems were bidding against one another; the assistants at once left them the field, and it was soon knocked off to the banker at two hundred dollars. Like many another smart man, the banker thought he could tell whether any "cappers" were being used at the sale or not. And like many another smart man, he never suspected that he was himself being used as one. But he was an old acquaintance of the owner of the property. Now, if there is any man on earth who is kind and considerate to an old friend from the East, it is the man who has lived a few months in California. A man whom you knew in the East as a mere speaking acquaintance seems like a long-lost brother, provided you have real estate to sell. In fact a speaking acquaintance is not always necessary. You may have cut him there for some very good reason, but all the same when he comes here your arms naturally open to renew the acquaintance, provided always that he has some money. The feeling of the other is very analogous. You seem to him like an American in a foreign country; and if he ever knew you as a man who has made some money some time, he reposes in you much of the same trustful confidence that you would in a fellow-countryman in the wilds of the Congo. The owner of the property had soon discovered that the banker was in town, and had told him, if he saw anything nice at the auction that showed any prospect of turning a few honest dollars before he returned to the East, to bid it off and hold it for a rise. He need not pay a cent on it, but merely write a check in such a way that it would be worthless, and hand it in to the clerk of the auctioneer. Such things were necessary for appearance's sake, but he would see that the check was destroyed. Nothing can cement the renewal of an old friendship like such an offer as this. Your modern rich man is tickled with such concession to his greatness. No one would think of making such an offer to a poor man, not even to a poor relation. But it is the right of the rich man to pick up a few dollars at the expense of some one else without risking a cent of his own money.

Bidding now became more spirited, and some small fry began to buy. But Mr. Brown and the watery-eyed man still kept aloof. Several lots were sold at from one hundred and seventy-five to one hundred and eighty-five dollars, when banker Squeems startled the crowd by bidding in a lot for one hundred and seventy, and announcing that he would take the rest of the block at the same price. The auctioneer, who was getting a fat commission on the gross amount of the genuine sales, smiled internally, and was about to offer another lot when the owner of the property suddenly pulled him down by the coat-tail and took him one side.

"What the duce are you at?" whispered the owner. "That is old Squeems, one of the richest bankers in the West. Get up an excuse to adjourn for lunch right away. Have the Major scrape acquaintance with him, and introduce him to some of the crowd. It won't do for you or me to be seen talking with him."

An intermission for lunch soon followed, during which those who came with the full intention of buying nothing crowded out more actual buyers, upset more coffee, soiled more sandwiches, and broke more crockery than all the rest. During lunch it was noised about that the richest banker in Chicago, and the richest beer brewer in Milwaukee, and Mr. Mason, one of the most successful manufacturers in St. Louis, were among the principal buyers. Though Mr. Brown pricked up his ears at the mention of the two latter names he still maintained nobly the exclusiveness of his exalted station. But Western men are less exclusive, and Mr. Mason introduced himself to banker Squeems, and banker Squeems, who had already introduced himself to Herr Katzenjammer (because being rich and living on the same lake they felt like neighbors), introduced him to Herr K.; wealth being a sufficient foundation for mutual confidence and mutual admiration. The three stood in a triangle after lunch, Mr. Mason sitting on the head of his cane picking his teeth with his knife, while a diamond sparkled on his extended little finger; banker Squeems, in deep meditation, trying to dig out a gopher with the toe of his boot; and Herr K., with his thumbs in his vest pockets, fondling with his fingers the dome of his abdomen. It was unanimously agreed by the triumvirate that the property was all right, that Los Angeles was certain to be a large city, and this addition was to be one of the finest portions of the whole. A ring of listeners had gathered around them drinking in the weighty wisdom they dispensed, on the outskirts of which Mr. Brown and the watery-eyed man, who was a capitalist from New York, lingered with aristocratic exclusiveness.

As the triumvirate decided the fate of the city, and the land generally, a dozen or more people in the surrounding crowd began to look over the country around them, and to discover that there was something in California besides climate. A capitalist from Boston suddenly remembered that he had seen some orange-groves somewhere near by, and another recollected that out of the car-window he had seen something that might have been fields of grain. Banker Squeems passed a favorable judgment on the soil that he was upturning with his foot, and soon a dozen others were scratching up some of it; and a solid old lawyer from Philadelphia, who didn't know beans from barley, pronounced it a very suitable soil for oranges.

"I am really ashamed of this morning's work," said the auctioneer as he mounted the stand again after lunch. "I have spent the better part of my life in trying to lead men to higher things. I regret to say that, owing to the perversity of human nature, I made a failure of it in one line. But I am bound to succeed, and if I can't do better in my present calling there will be nothing left for me but to turn hangman, in which case I shall be most happy to officiate for any of you gentlemen with whom I can't succeed to-day. Do your duty now, and we'll close out this batch of lots quicker than a squaw can knock out a watermelon."

"Do you really want that, my dear?" said the watery-eyed man to his wife as a fine corner was offered.

"Oh yes! Do buy it. I think it is just lovely here."

"You know I am always glad to do anything to please you, and if we should lose the money it won't ruin us. But if we are going to risk anything at all we might as well have a piece large enough to be of some use in case the investment should turn out well," he said.

Whereupon he began to bid. Instead of offering an inside lot with the privilege of the corner at the same price, the auctioneer, who with the owner, had been gauging the verdancy of the crowd during lunch, had now offered a corner with the privilege of buying the next two inside lots at the same price. The watery-eyed man seated himself broadly in the trap, bid off the corner at a hundred and ninety-five dollars, and took the next two lots at the same figure.

From this time until sundown sales were rapid, and when the auction closed one fifth of the property had been sold to genuine buyers for more than the owner had paid for the whole of it. But Mr. Brown remained obdurately wrapped in his individuality. He had reached the conclusion that the property would some day be valuable, but at present he had no use for it.

The sale of the property was continued from the map at the office of the owner in town. And next morning the lower limbs of Mr. Brown in some mysterious manner carried him in his morning walk directly toward the office. He saw a number of genuine buyers gathered around the map, and they wore such good clothes and looked so much like men of means, that he felt a violent inclination to go in and see what they were doing. He was still quite certain that he did not want to buy. He was only curious to know how the property was selling. So in he walked.

He found several purchasers of the day before not only completing their payments but buying more lots. And it was evident that none of them had yet had time to see the abstract of title to the land, or even cared to see it, though it was announced that it was at the office of one of the leading attorneys, with his opinion attached to it. After staring at the crowd for a few minutes Mr. Brown made the further discovery that new parties were buying, and buying lots too of which they not only knew nothing about the title, but which they had not even seen, and knew nothing about the location of, except from the map. They were genuine buyers, so well satisfied that they did not care about either title or location.

While Mr. Brown was watching the buyers with increasing interest, and coming to the conclusion that the property must be something unusually good to make such well-dressed people in such haste to get some of it, Herr Katzenjammer, who had been duly breakfasted and shaved at the hour becoming a man of wealth on his travels, waddled into the office, and concluded that he would take a few more lots adjoining those he had bought. Banker Squeems, who had happened in a few minutes before, and was looking over the map, pulled the owner aside, and in a low voice said,

"I really like this town, and believe those lots are a good investment. I will take them to keep, and pay up on them if you will let me in on the cellar-floor. You know I bid pretty high on them yesterday so as to help you out a little."

"It wouldn't do, you know, to lower the price," said the owner, gently stroking his chin. "But I can of course allow you a commission on the sale to yourself, the same as if you had found me another buyer for them."

The eyes of the banker brightened at once; for if there is anything that pleases the modern millionaire in a boom, it is the recognition of his importance involved in "letting him in on the commission." So the trade was quickly made by allowing twenty per cent discount on the price, and calling it a commission. Mr. Katzenjammer opened his eyes as he saw the banker buying some more lots, as he supposed; and their expansion was increased by seeing Mr. Mason, who had just come in, violently interested in the part of the map adjoining the lots bought by the banker. Herr K. waddled out into an adjoining saloon and ingulfed two schooners of beer, waddled into the office again and looked around awhile, waddled out and swamped a third schooner at a single gulp, then came in and bought half a block next the block the banker had taken.

Mr. Mason now delivered himself of the very sage remark, that if one is going to gamble on these things at all, one might as well have enough to make something on in case one wins, and told the owner that if he would change the lots he had bought the day before to another block, he would take half of the block. The owner consented very reluctantly, because the block Mason wanted was "extra choice," and he really didn't care to sell any more of the best blocks at present prices. At least so he said. But he also added that he always liked to please his first customers, because they were more appreciative. Whereupon Mr. Mason took the rest of the block of which the brewer had bought half.

"A very much better investment than it seemed at first. Very fine property. But on the whole I would as soon have my money in dry-goods on my shelves in New Yawk," remarked Mr. Brown to himself as he walked out.

The next day saw him at the office again watching new people buy. The general opinion of the buyers was that the property was the very finest in the city, and as over two hundred lots had been sold since the auction, prices would certainly advance in a day or two.

" It's all right, I know," said Mr. Brown, as he walked out. "But dry-goods in New Yawk are good enough for me."

The next day found him at the office again. He felt a strange interest in the outcome of the sale for which he could not account. The excitement was increasing some, for it was said that the brick were already on the ground for a new schoolhouse which the owner was going to build at once and give to the city, and that he had already made a contract with the gas and water companies to extend their mains to the tract, and that he was now busily figuring with the street-car company to have the road extended there. Mr. B. felt more interested than ever, but nevertheless he walked out, making to himself some remark about " dry-goods in New Yawk." He didn't hear the owner call " the Major " into his back room and tell him to "put the Colonel onto that beer vat. Run him down to his hotel to-night, and give him three hundred for his bargain, and go him five if necessary."

While inwardly vowing that "dry-goods in New Yawk" were the safest of all investments, Mr. Brown was nevertheless propelled by his legs the next morning to the real-estate office a little faster than usual.

Mr. Katzenjammer, clad in ruby smile, stood in the doorway, fondly patting his stomach with his fat fingers.

"Vell, I make already my exshpenses on dot leetle shpeclation," he said.

"What! have you sold already?" inquired Mr. Brown with eyes wide open.

"O yaas. I only buy 'em shoost to make a leetle durn. I always like to make my exshpenses venn I traffuls. I cleant oop fife hoondert dollar. I make some more yet before I go home." Whereupon he waddled off to a beer-saloon, leaving Mr. Brown in wonder over this new phase of business. He had thought he knew all about making money. But the idea of a man on his travels making the expenses of his trip out of the country he is visiting, and with scarcely the turning of his finger, was something ravishingly unique. And why could not he, a great and successful trader, do it as well as this coarse, ignorant man from the West, who knew "nothing but beer, even if he is rich"? So thought Mr. Brown as he walked in.

"I didn't get them a bit too quick," said one of two men to the other as they passed Mr. Brown in the doorway coming out. They are selling like the deuce on the outside now, and I overheard the General telling the Commodore that he was going to raise prices at twelve o'clock."

Mr. Brown went in and watched the crowd for a little while. When he came out he had nothing to say about dry-goods in New York. A serious air of business mingled with a smile of gratification was on his face, and he murmured softly to himself, "While I am about it, I can just as well make my wife's expenses at the same time."

CHAPTER V.

THE SMILE OF THE NATIVE.

SOMBER tints began to overrun the land, the grain-fields and the wild-oats were yellowing far and wide, the alfileria and clovers covered with a deep, brown mat of rich fodder the slopes they so lately carpeted with brilliant green, and with them in the embrace of death lay the spangled host of poppies, pinks, violets, and other early flowers. The summer of 1886 was coming, and with it an increasing number of strangers. People who a year before had gone back with contempt for everything in California, led by some strange impulse were now every day returning and buying property at two or three times what they could have bought it for the year before. With them came another class—people who had been here before and liked the country and climate, but who could not afford to give up the good business they had at home, or else could not leave their many friends and live so far away. The second or third year sees many of them back with the proceeds of the business that they have sold out, and the friends are left to shift for themselves. Others come and spend a few weeks, and go away with no definite impressions of any kind. The next season sees them back, lingering farther into the spring, and saying:

"I don't know exactly what it is, but there is something about this that I kind o' like."

If they come back the third season they are quite certain to become fixtures. These classes have gone far toward building up California, and they now came faster than ever. With them came capitalists, speculators, real-estate agents, and adventurers; also a goodly crop of invalids and tourists, with farmers and others looking for land upon which to make an easy living and have some money over at the end of the year.

But the majority cared nothing about the solid resources of the land, and were looking only for amusement or a chance to make some money without work. For the news was already widely spread in the East that the land was "booming," and it was more widely spread by the papers in all directions. There were still many who felt nothing but contempt for a country they did not understand and that they did not try to understand; but the majority were on the other extreme, and finding the land rapidly growing, with crops all good and money plenty, fell at once into blind, unreasoning love with it. Hence a rapid increase in the letters, already too abundant and silly, sent to Eastern papers. East, West, North and South, Southern California was absurdly overpraised in a grand splash of adjectives and adverbs idiotically substituted for nouns and verbs by a batch of men and women who had never before set foot beyond a pavement, and did not know enough to write facts even if they had wanted to. And the worst of the lot were those specially sent out by the large Eastern periodicals because they are "disinterested." Such correspondents, knowing nothing about the country, and having no time to learn anything about it, even if they had had sense enough, judged the land only by its pace of prosperity, and with their absurd praise did it more harm than if they had stayed at home.

And the summer of 1886 came on,—at least the almanac said so,—and the indigo of the larkspur was deepening over the slopes where the golden light of the primrose had burned away, and tulips of lavender and tulips of golden hue, with the bright-eyed iris, and the purple and pink of the penstemon and blue phacelias, were rising above the grave of the little blue lily and the shooting-star. Day after day the sun climbed a cloudless arch, and fresh and cool the unfailing breeze came bounding inland from over the blue billows of the Pacific. And to the surprise of all the coming of the stranger was more rapid than ever, and his satisfaction with all he found was greater than ever. As had always been the case, the summer pleased the new-comers more than the winter. The well-known fact that San Francisco is uncomfortably cool in summer might have taught them that the same cause—the Arctic current in the ocean—might make the coast a few hundred miles south about right. But it is too much trouble to reason about such things, and the surprise one feels in finding this coast so much cooler in summer than the East makes many a one fall at once in love with it.

By the middle of the summer Los Angeles was growing at the rate of about a thousand a month, and San Diego at the rate of about five hundred a month. The deposits in the banks were already several times the amount of the capital stock, and gold was more plenty on the streets than silver in ordinary times. For property was selling every day in all directions, and selling generally for cash; the time of buying on a large margin having not yet arrived, except in a few places where the auction system was already in use.

Santa Barbara and Ventura counties were growing slowly, but still steadily and in a substantial way, with no excitement. Orange County, then a part of Los Angeles County, was growing somewhat faster, but as yet with no excitement or nonsense. San Bernardino County was growing still faster, but upon a perfectly sound basis. People there looked upon the stranger as a valuable dispensation, but placed no dependence upon his continued coming; relieved him joyfully of his surplus gold, and put it into waterworks and other things to develop the productive power of the soil instead of wasting it in mere conveniences for strangers yet to come. Nearly all its growth was upon ten- and twenty- acre tracts—the peculiar kind of settlement that in San Bernardino and Los Angeles counties had been going on for years by wealthy people, and which had really started the boom.

The impression is general that the Californians worked up the boom. Nothing could be farther from the truth. Such a thing would have been quite impossible, even if they had been foolish enough to attempt it. Some had indeed been advertising the resources of the land in various ways, and many were anxious to see new settlers come in and develop the country. But they wanted men who would work and improve and produce something, and not men who would merely raise land values and cut up the country into town lots, and turn away the attention of people from production, and actually decrease production until they had to buy from abroad what they could better raise themselves. But the majority of those having land to sell were stockmen who wanted no development of any kind that would impair the free range on government land, or old fossils who wanted no progress that would increase taxes on their holdings of wild land, or people who had been trying so long in vain to sell that they had given up the idea in disgust, or those who were still full of the old ideas that the country was of no value anyhow, and had been too lazy or too stupid to travel about and learn that the world had moved in the years they had been sitting in the shade smoking cigarettes.

To all such the rapid buying and building was

a grand surprise, and probably no such smiles were ever seen on earth as those they exchanged around the corner after pocketing the money of the "tenderfoot;" excepting always, nevertheless, the smile of a year later when they had come to the conclusion that the aforesaid "tenderfoot" was going to make too much money out of them, and bought him out for ten or fifteen times what he had paid them.

So far the boom, though aided by an occasional auction, and the efforts of Eastern boomers, who were rapidly coming in, was quite spontaneous. Property in all directions was changing hands, and prices were slowly rising. But it was all good property; prices were not extravagant; and in only a few places were they at all ahead of what the stage of settlement would justify.

Week after week rolled on, and still the people came. The clatter of harvest machinery died away along the plains, the hum of the bee ceased along the hills, and the new-comers bought faster than ever. The soft glow of purple and rose that had lingered around the mountain tops under the declining sun of summer had faded out, and they now lay asleep in a golden haze. Along the bottom-lands the bright pink of the sand-verbena was vanishing, and among the chink of the rocks the mimulus was closing its scarlet trumpets. Even the sunflower in the shady dells was preparing to retire for the season, and the crimson of the silene and the tender blue of the mints and lupins that overspread the slopes in summer were already gone. The almanac said that autumn had come, but the "tenderfoot" came faster than ever. It seemed, too, that he had more money than ever, and had come here for the express purpose of finding a place to locate it. And though the openings for it increased fast enough to please any reasonable creature, he acted as if he had never before had an opportunity to convert gold into real estate, and wanted to make up for lost time as quickly as possible. Diamonds now began to sparkle on bosoms that had never before known starch. The silk hat beamed over many a fossiliferous skull, and shining new buggies dashed here and there with real-estate speculators and agents who for years had gone afoot.

Weeks rolled on, and the sea-breeze died away to a gentle breath, the air became drier and drier, along the hills the heteromeles hung out its brilliant clusters of scarlet berries, the golden-rod was aglow in the meadows, and the feathery bloom of the baccharis drifted over with white large portions of the chapparal, and still the people came faster than ever, and bought and built and paid higher prices, and seemed more happy than ever in their bargains. And over the canvas the newspaper correspondent flung his paint-pots of adjectives more lavishly and recklessly than ever, and Eastern editors believed his extravagant nonsense, and wrote editorials that still farther increased the number of crazy pilgrims, and a war in railroad rates accelerated their rapid pace.

The still bright days rolled on, the nights became cooler, the robin and blue-bird came down from the high mountains, the burnished green of the maillard's head shone in the lagoon, the silvery "honk" of the wild-goose fell softly from the sky, the almanac said that winter had come, and still the crowd increased. And the natives stood lost in wonder, for the Holidays were not yet past, and after the Holidays is the time when the great body of the tourists always comes.

The Holidays came and washed the land with abundant rain, and though some of the invalids were mad, and swore that the climate was a fraud and that all men were liars because the long stream of sunshine had been broken for a few days, the great majority of the new-comers were more pleased than ever. For daily fresh tints of green brightened over hill and dale, and beneath the warm sun the land, with its new buildings rising on every hand, looked never so prosperous. And daily the smile brightened on the face of the hotel-keeper, and real-estate agent and speculator, and land-owner of high and low degree; for faster and faster on every train came more men and more money.

Heretofore, though too many had been buying for speculation only, there had been little real gambling. But now hundreds who had bought only to improve began to buy something to hold for a rise; and hundreds more, who so far had bought nothing, now began to think they might as well make some money as see other people make it. Prices were rising almost by the day, any kind of property could be quickly sold at an advance, and the number of those who had made a handsome "clean-up" on a small investment was already very large. And still the funniest part of the whole was to see the number of people—people, too, largely from the land of booms, and others, who had traveled far and wide yet had never seen a boom. No, I am mistaken again:

the funniest part was to see the number of those who had seen booms before, and thought they were now wise enough to know where the top of the next one was.

When the boom started the Californians laughed at it. The first stage was spontaneous and healthy. The crazy part of it was started by professional boomers flocking in from Kansas City, Chicago, St. Paul, San Francisco, and other places, and showing the natives how to make money out of wind. Never were more apt scholars found, and they soon became dizzy with the rapid instillation of wisdom. Farmers began to neglect their farms and go into town-lot speculation. Orchards and vineyards were given over to the malva and wild-mustard, and too many bore only crops of town-lot stakes. It became far more dignified for the owner of town-lots that were advancing in value by the day to buy his eggs from Iowa, his chickens from Kansas City, his pork from Chicago, and his butter from the north, than to bother with raising them. If you met a granger on his way to town it was a safe bet that he was going in to buy a sack of potatoes imported from Humboldt County, in the far north. And all this was aggravated by the fact that it was now quite useless to talk to a new-comer about buying a farm. Of the hundreds who came with the intention of buying productive land, not one in a hundred could be induced to look at a piece. Why buy a farm now when it was so much better to double one's money first on town-lots and then buy a farm? These were the sages who spread out their money as thin as possible in buying town-lots on a small margin, lost the whole of it, and then went back to tell Eastern editors that the whole of Southern California was cut up into twenty-five-foot lots.

Before the winter of 1886-7 nearly everything sold as town-lots was in additions to cities already well established, and where it was plain that something of a city would always exist. But now began the laying out of new cities—cities made to order, of which the principal resources were climate and scenery. Why should the owner of two such conditions trouble himself with any such gross materialities as trade? Was not the whole country growing with a rapid and substantial growth, extending over town and country and covering a vast area? Was it not certain that the whole East was running as fast as it could away from the horrors of its climate? No such growth had ever before been seen in any part of the world, and would have been impossible anywhere except under the climate of Southern California, which has for years infatuated a certain proportion of its visitors, and will continue to infatuate them to the end of time. What wonder, then, that Farmer Smith or Granger Jones should think that the farm where the rabbits had for so many years kept him and his family from starvation had just the finest bit of climate and scenery on earth, and that several thousand people must soon need a slice of it?

Yet amid all this nonsense the land was quietly filling as it is to-day, and as it was before the boom, with people who neither knew nor cared anything about booms. Quietly as snowflakes they were settling over the land, ignored and laughed at as a lot of innocents by their wiser brethren who did not purpose taking a lifetime to get rich.

CHAPTER VI.

AND AGAIN THE NATIVE SMILES.

ONCE more the cooing of the dove came from the sycamores along the creeks and the carol of the oriole from the live-oak groves, the pink of the gentian and the scarlet bracts of the painted cup rose above the spangled green that robed the plain, and along the hills the golden light of the rock-rose and the wild alfalfa illumined the grayish green of the ramiria and sage. The almanac said that the spring of 1887 had come, and with it came an increase in the number of wealthy strangers that beggared fondest expectations. New varieties of fools arrived on every train, and every new variety of folly seemed more contagious than the last. The streets were everywhere crowded, gold clinked on every hand, and imaginary millionaires by the score rode around the streets in shining new buggies with fast horses, or bustled about the banks and real-estate offices with check-books sticking from their outside breast-pockets,

The crimson bugles of the wild gooseberry lit up the delicate lavender of the lilac, and the creamy trumpets of the wild honeysuckle hung over the red limbs and bright-green leaves of the manzanita; lower down the lupin and the vetch scattered their carmine and purple along the base of the hills, and the marigold and the chilla were spreading their lemon and blue over the slopes below, and still the travel increased, and the more wealthy and reckless the new-comers were. Speculation in outside town-sites was now in full career. No longer any need of the brass band or free lunch or glib-tongued auctioneer or assistants of any kind. Though all such were still freely used they were quite superfluous. No longer any need of guarantees of railroads, waterworks, colleges, hotels, or anything else. No longer any need of abstracts of title, showing the property, or even setting stakes to mark the lots. All that was now necessary was a big map with so many lots marked off with red chalk to mean "Sold," a big notice in the window "Prices raised twenty per cent to-morrow," plenty of printed forms of contracts of sale, and plenty of clerks to fill them out. Little it mattered where the land lay. North, south, east, or west, in a hole or on a hill, it was all the same to the man who never saw it, never wanted to see it, and never expected to go near it, but did expect to sell it to some other ass in thirty days for twice what he had paid for it. It was now no trouble to sell anything that was chopped into twenty-five-foot lots. No matter whether there were any farming land around it or any reason for the existence of a town there for the next century; all that was necessary was a sufficient acreage chopped up fine enough.

Of what use is a twenty-five-foot lot to any one? was a question that few asked. But after all, who is the wiser?—the man who says, "This is all nonsense, and can't last," or the man who says, "My dear sir, I know all that as well as you do. But when the world takes a notion to be an ass, it is for a while the biggest ass in the universe. The man who caters the soonest to its morbid appetite is the smartest fellow. In a boom you can sell two twenty-five-foot lots for considerably more than you can sell one fifty-foot lot. Smart folks who think they know all about human nature, think they know better than this. But you will please remember that neither Solomon nor Shakespeare ever saw a first-class boom."

Be all this as it may, the Eastern people, who

afterward complained the most about it, were the most to blame for the small-lot business. There never was a better illustration of the old adage, "One fool makes many." The natives at first sneered at it, Eastern boomers started it, Eastern fools did the first buying, and by their success finally turned the heads of the Californians themselves, and made of them the biggest fools of the lot. The plain fact is, that those parts where nothing less than fifty-foot lots were sold did no better than where they were all twenty-five.

During almost the whole of the year 1887 this kind of work went steadily on. Tens of thousands of acres, fit only for grain, hay, alfalfa, or pasture, were thus mangled and sold to people of whom not one in a thousand expected ever to use the lots, but bought them only to sell to some one else in sixty days at a good advance. And yet scarcely any one of these paper town-sites could fairly be called a swindle. The soil was almost invariably good, the location healthy, the scenery and climate first-class, and the title either perfect, or quickly made so by the buyer paying in full. A mere boy who buys property anywhere, not with the intention of using it but of selling to some one else at an advance in a few weeks, should have sense enough to know that he is gambling, and keep quiet if he loses. And yet thousands of successful business men from the East plunged headlong into this game, and then went home to set up a world-wide howl. Nor is it exactly fair to call robbery even the outrageous rents that now prevailed. When a dozen persons are trying to rent his new building before the first brick of its foundation is laid, who can be expected to sit calmly down and calculate the tenant's profit on the lease?

The success of some of these paper town-sites was wonderful. Thousands of acres bought for thirty, twenty, and even ten dollars an acre, and, without water for irrigation, worth not half of those figures, were sold in lots at from one thousand to ten thousand dollars an acre. And this was done in dozens of places, and continued for many months, with the buyers becoming daily more ravenous. At many a sale of the merest trash buyers stood in line all night, and fifty dollars, and even a hundred, were often paid for places in the line in the morning. Incredible as such statements may appear, they were as nothing to the private offers made and refused. The instances in which two fools met would fill a volume much larger than this. Were I to give a few in which the names of men widely known throughout the United States as embodiments of shrewdness, financial wisdom, and business ability figured as parties, the credibility of this whole book would be destroyed at once.

Yet it must not be supposed that a town-lot craze was all there was of it. There were instances enough to prove that he who flatters himself that any amount of experience, business ability, or financial shrewdness will enable him to hold the helm steady in such a storm of example as here overwhelmed the new-comer, has something yet to learn about himself. But if it had been a mere following of leaders over an empty sea, the canvas would soon have been hauled in. It is true enough that the great majority of buyers were only following each other. "What *sheep* these mortals be," should have read the California edition of Shakespeare for those times. Yet there was enough of solidity in it all to keep it up to a certain point; for actual settlers were coming at a more rapid rate than ever, and making great and permanent improvements all over the land. Most of them settled in the cities, and the settlement of the productive part of the land was temporarily retarded. But nearly all of them came to stay, though thousands were destined afterward to wring their living from the soil they at first despised, and thus become an important factor in the future prosperity of the country. And so the whole was growing more rapidly than ever, and with a class of settlers that no other part of the United States has ever yet seen or is likely ever to see. Los Angeles was now growing at the rate of about two thousand a month and San Diego at the rate of about a thousand, while Pasadena, Monrovia, and other towns were increasing at the same pace. And *still* the funniest part of the whole was to see the number of people alleged to be intelligent, and people who claimed to have traveled, yet had never before seen a boom. Excuse me—I am wrong again. The funniest thing was, continuously, to see the number of people who had seen booms before and been through them and lost money on them, and who were now in position from their past experience to know *exactly* where the next one would stop.

And now the old-timers who a year ago had gone around the corner and laughed in their sleeves after unloading on the "tenderfoot" the lots or acres over which for many a year they had groaned when the time for paying a few dollars of taxes came around, went around the corner again. But this time the smile of other days sat not upon their faces. A sad and serious look had taken its place.

"What? *Jeeee*rusalem! Shall I, who have lived on beans and peppers and rustled clams these many years on the salt-sea shore so as to hold my lots, now see some rich old duffer from the East get still richer at my expense?

"Shall I, who have chewed jerky these many years and never could afford to eat a decent beefsteak out of my own cattle, now see the stranger drinking champagne out of the profits of the land I sold him at a sacrifice because I was fool enough to think he was paying me more than I thought it was worth?

"Shall I, who for years have tried to sell those blasted lots for enough to pay the fare for myself and family out of the town, and couldn't do it, now get left, with only a few thousand dollars?

"Not much! I haven't skinned dead cattle to save their hides in dry years, and drunk mescal instead of good whisky, for nothing. We never knew what the cussed country was worth until outsiders found it out, and now we are green enough to let them make all the money out of it."

And so they reasoned here and there. The man who for years had run a successful cactus ranche compared notes with the ex-tar-weed rancher, and both came to the conclusion that the stranger was walking off with entirely too much of the "swag." And the real-estate man who for years had gazed at the vacant doorway of his office waiting for a second Tom Scott to bring a transcontinental railroad, and the man who for as long a time had been driving his sheep over his neighbor's range to steal feed enough to enable him to pay the light taxes on his own range, both reached the same conclusion. All of them now had plenty of money, and as the banks were full of the strangers' coin, which they were quite willing to loan to the solid old citizens at fifteen per cent, the aforesaid solid old citizens had little difficulty in rescuing enough of the precious soil from the hand of the unworthy stranger.

But if paid for in full the money would not go far enough, and too much of the profit of the great future would pass into the hand of the "tenderfoot," instead of passing into the hands of those who had borne the heat and burden of the long day. Hence they followed the now almost universal custom—bought on contract, with a payment of only one fourth or one third down, and a personal obligation to pay the remainder in six and twelve months, with interest at twelve per cent. And so the old-timers bought in again at from five to fifteen times the price at which they had sold a year before, and again they went around the corner and smiled in their sleeves at the way in which they had again taken in the "tenderfoot."

CHAPTER VII.

HIGH TIDE OF THE BOOM.

THE mantles of white that robed the tops of the higher mountains were fast becoming tattered along the edges; wee little quails fluttered in squealing lines of gray from the brush along the road-sides; the soft tints of the choryzanthe tinged the lower hills with pink; the silken floss of the dodder tangled the wild buckwheat in a maze of orange light, and the snowy bloom of the elder outshone along the low lands that of the sumac along the hills. Summer had come again, and still the stream of travel enlarged, and almost by the day the proportion of wealthy fish in it increased. And they bit at the barest hook more recklessly than ever. Though many of the old-timers were buying in again, there were still lots enough thrown on the market from every point of the compass to feed the most ravenous of the school of gudgeons.

Did ever such a flock of such luscious goslings

so insist on flying into the mouth of the fox? With nine tenths of those now coming such little trifles as resources were of no moment. All they knew or cared to know was that people who had made money were buying, and that prices were almost daily rising. Many were tourists of the class who travel solely for hotels. The hotel, its table, and its service are about all they see in any country, and about all they have to talk about when they go away. From these they form their estimate of any new country. California now had good hotels, and all of this class were pleased. With the exception of the ancient Missions and a few broken-down adobe buildings, old enough to pass for antiquities, the hotels and the real-estate offices were all they saw.

Time was when the countryman cut a ridiculous figure in the city. But to-day every "Country Jake" knows all about the city, while so many city people now travel so exclusively by rail and fill up the time between stations with cards or novels, that the proportion of those that are lost the moment they set foot beyond the pavement is greater than ever. Whether sausages grow on trees, or underground, like potatoes, they hardly know nor care. The genuine

City Jake, as he performed in California at this time, was enough to turn the head of any one. The less he knew or cared about the substantial resources of the land, and the less competent he was to judge of them, even if he had tried to, the more recklessly he bought. What, therefore, was more natural than for the residents, new as well as old, to ask: " Where is all this going to end? Are we all fools, or are we not? Do we know anything, or don't we?" He who thinks that under such a strain he could have answered any of these questions soberly and correctly would probably have been the biggest fool of the lot if he had been here.

" Don't it beat the dickens?" said Major Muffin to Judge Bumps, a lawyer who had given up a good practice to go into real estate.

" Why, we are just taking a tumble to ourselves. I knew long ago that we were going to beat San Francisco, only I was green enough to think it would take eight or ten years to do it."

" How long do you think this is going to last?" inquired Judge Dumble of Colonel Gote.

" Last? Why we are just settling down to business. The world is just finding out about our climate."

"Marvelous, isn't it?" said General Applehead to Commodore Shadtail.

"Not at all. The only marvel is that it has been so long coming," replied the Commodore, flapping against his leg a new check-book with which he had just come out of the bank. "We have just struck our gait: before, we have been only scoring."

"This is now the central point of a thousand converging lines from every town, city, and hamlet in the United States," said General Theophilus Turkeytail, who had made three millions on the boom, looking down with the air of a big St. Bernard, examining a little whiffet of a man who had made only half a million out of nothing. "She is going now by her own momentum, Sir. We have sixty millions on this side of the Atlantic, Sir, and when they are exhausted there are lots more on the other side."

And the smaller millionaire looked gratefully up into the great, wise countenance, drew a long breath of satisfaction, and went off to buy something more on credit, to increase his load when the day of reckoning came.

"I always knew it would be so," said General Spraddlebuck, who for several years before the boom had been vainly trying to sell his town-lots for one fourth of what they cost him ten years before, so as to be able to go to another town, but who was now, according to one of the papers, a great "enterprising and progressive citizen, whose undying faith in our beautiful city has made him rich.'

"We have thought at times that we were going too fast, but we have been merely trembling at the shadow of our own greatness," said the Rev. Solomon Sunrise, who on week-days had been more successful in getting a cheap option on a piece of valuable property than in beating the devil out of an immortal soul on Sundays. "We have but girded our loins for the race, and are running now like a strong man rejoicing in his strength, knowing no fear." Whereupon the Rev. Solomon felt for his check-book, and walked off to complete a good trade he had just made.

And thus they reasoned almost everywhere. And indeed there was some ground for such reasoning among the thousands who knew nothing of the immense amount of good land, good climate, and fine scenery to be found in Southern

California, the supply of which must inevitably break the market, even though the demand were fifty times what it now was.

Yet never was there such an opportunity for men of moderate ambition and a little caution to lay up a competency on so small an investment. Up to a certain limit the game was certain for all who came in soon enough. Hundreds played it in this way, and are comfortable to-day on an investment of only a few hundred dollars, and often on an investment of nothing but time and energy. But few could realize that making a few thousand dollars with a few hundred is an opportunity that one meets scarcely once in a lifetime, and that the chances in any given case are heavily against it. Nor could many see that the very fact that one can double money in a few weeks and often in a few days proves the existence of a state of affairs on the continuance of which for even a single day no one can safely bet. But few thought of such things; and few, even of those who could on any day in 1887 have sold out for a handsome fortune made out of almost nothing but wind, had sense enough to give some unincumbered property to wife or children. The most of them drove blindly on, in full confidence that prices would continue rising to the point they desired, and then be kind enough to give them due notice of their intention to stop.

The rich people, who at this time overran the land, were alleged to be intelligent. And so they were, as intelligence of the day goes. Most of them had received a fine newspaper education. But even a newspaper education will not enable one to make money at real-estate speculation, if he studies the situation only in the papers and from the windows of a Pullman car. And the man who travels by special car is worse yet. By a violent effort a man of considerable wealth can sometimes be got as far as five miles away from an ordinary sleeping-car. But the man who can drag a nabob more than a mile away from the soft cushions and the dinner-table of his private car is the smartest chap of the day. What wonder, then, that in a land so different from everything the Eastern man has ever seen he should entirely overlook all the true resources and lavish all his attention on the most worthless part? It seems incredible, but is absolute truth, that the only really valuable part of the land, outside of established business centers in established cities, never had any boom, and rose scarcely any faster in price than it had risen for several years preceding. The lands that to-day are selling to wealthy settlers for cash, and selling faster than ever at from fifty to one hundred dollars an acre more than they brought during the height of the excitement, were then no attraction to the horde of wealthy speculators. These were the irrigable uplands before mentioned. Their settlement went steadily ahead as it had done before, but only a trifle faster, while all the riotous uproar was over dry land fit only for grain or common farming at the rate of a hundred and sixty acres to support a family, and over outside town-lots fit only for gambling on a rising market. The great groves of oranges that were paying from five hundred to a thousand dollars an acre, the vineyards of raisin-grapes that were paying two hundred, the orchards of apricots and other fruits that were paying from one hundred to one hundred and fifty an acre, not one in a hundred even went to look at.

Nor did one in a thousand care to know if there were any similar conditions near by lying undeveloped—land and water that money could bring together. Hundreds of thousands of acres of the best fruit-land in the world lay unsought and unsuspected by them, with water enough in the near mountains to irrigate it; yet scarcely one of them could be induced to listen to the few who talked of land and water instead of advancing prices, commercial advantages, climate, transcontinental railroads, steamship lines from China and Japan, or anything but the simplest and best proved means of producing wealth from the soil; means that would be sure to hold if all else failed. It was only upon these lands that the kind of settlement was found that made Southern California what it was, and distinguished it from a mere farming country; and it was their rapid settlement and the positive proof of the great profits to be obtained from them that started the boom and made possible its continuance. And now the evidence of their intrinsic value was on every hand, and the fruit buyers were constantly on the ground buying for cash anything and everything on the trees and vines, and picking and packing it themselves. And yet scarcely any turned aside to inquire into it. Indeed, the fact that the immense profits were dependent upon irrigation excited only the contempt of hundreds who consider irrigation a mere make-shift—a miserable substitute for rain—and do not know that dependence on the capricious clouds is the makeshift and irrigation is the solid work. Here and there a small tract of these lands was bought for a town-site, but the greater part of them was passed contemptuously by the noble army of buyers.

The absurd prices to which town-lots and dry land had risen would alone have caused a great reaction, but other causes were at work. Everywhere the newspapers and people of one section were saying something mean about every other section, and everything of the kind was greedily copied and applied without discrimination to the whole State by the editors of Eastern papers, especially in the blizzard- and cyclone-ridden sections, where the drain of people and money into California was most felt.

The tone of the greater part of the correspondence of Eastern papers was now also quite different from what it had been. Many correspondents were honestly deprecating the extravagance to which the boom had been carried, but many more had a stronger reason, quite unsuspected by the innocent editors who published their letters; and those who had sent out special correspondents, because they were disinterested and "old reliables," often fared no better. Seing the land prosperous, with gold glittering in every palm, and plain mud making more in five minutes' work than genius could harvest in a month, it was quite natural for genius to inquire, "What is there in this for me?" The next step was generally to wait on some town-site proprietor, president of a land company, Chamber of Commerce, or citizens' committee, and offer to write up the enterprise or section or town for a consideration commensurate with its importance and the lofty ideas of the times. The correspondent who thought the fate of the country was in his hands, too often thought it was smart to intimate what the nature of the "write up" might be in case its value were not appreciated at a proper money standard. If so, he was quite likely to retire from the office sadder and madder than when he entered. Often he had the impudence to attempt to do up the country on a few hours' acquaintance, and fared little better than in the other case. In either case he poured out venom to the full capacity of his still, and this was quickly copied by scores of Eastern papers whose editors thought that praise of California was getting rather stale, and that readers would relish a change.

Several other things, quite unnoticed by the great majority of crazy speculators, were paving the way for a collapse. Although in town and country Southern California was growing at a pace wholly unprecedented in the United States, fully five sixths of the buyers were buying, not for use, but to sell at an advance to some one else in a few days or weeks. And as nearly all sales were upon contract, with only one fourth or one third paid in cash, the most of which amounted only to an option on the part of the buyer, the greater part of the property must inevitably be thrown back upon the market to save the first payment the moment prices ceased rising.

Taking as a basis almost anything now selling, except the irrigated lands before mentioned, the value of the three southern counties alone would have equaled the assessed value of the whole State. Nor did any one seem to see that there were already upon the market more town-lots than could be settled in ten years if every train were loaded with actual settlers. Another fact, quite unnoticed because the information was statistical and could be seen only by an examination of the records when too late, was that hundreds of the sales now made were made by strangers quietly unloading on the natives. But for this the stranger is entitled to no credit. He was as wild as the native, and yielded only to the enormous figures offered by the native, whom he had at last set crazy.

And now hundreds of farmers who had hitherto kept cool moved into town and went into town-lot speculation, while hundreds more who remained on their farms stopped raising anything to eat and bought nearly everything from abroad.

But the worst mistake was ignoring the immense amount of fine land and fine climate in Southern California, the supply of which must inevitably break any market at the present day. It was once a maxim that the best part of any country lies out of sight of the ordinary lines of travel, and especially out of sight of the railroad. But this seems to have been changed, and Southern California in particular is overrun with sages who think they see the whole of it by an occasional glance out of the car-window. The six southern counties contain over two million acres of fine arable land that under any sun would be pronounced first-class by any one who would take the trouble to examine it. On the driest half of this, one hundred and sixty acres will, without any irrigation whatever, afford as good a living as most Eastern farms of the same size. On the other half, one hundred and sixty acres, with the work and economy necessary the world over for successful farming, will give one a better living with more money over at the end of the year and less annoyance and climatic discomfort, than the same area in most of the Atlantic States. Then there are two millions more, which the last few years have proved the most valuable land in America when properly irrigated, and on the greater part of it water can be supplied. And upon the greater part of the first two millions the productive power can be increased by water to a degree quite inconceivable by those who have never seen the difference between absolute control of the water under a sun where things grow the whole year round, and dependence upon uncertain rainfall in a land where everything must grow in four or five months. And these four millions do not include any of the Colorado or Mojave deserts, which contain millions more awaiting the coming of water in the future. But few saw these facts, because it is so much easier to sit down and have an opinion than to travel about and learn something. And so nearly every one acted as if his own little section contained about all there was of good soil, climate, and scenery in

Southern California, made haste to secure all he could of it before it was too late, and did all he could to raise prices to a point that must inevitably break the market, no matter how great the actual merits of the property.

CHAPTER VIII.

GETTING OUT.

NEARLY every sale now made was genuine. At the public sales there were of course a few aids to correct judgment scattered judiciously among the crowd. It is doubtful if there are many real-estate sales in modern times without them. The man who thinks he is attending a sale where there are none, and is buying exclusively upon the standard set up by actual buyers, is liable to be a bigger goose than ever performed in California during the craziest time. Second-hand furniture can be trusted on its naked merits to bring at an auction more than it is worth. Second-hand horses often do even better. But one who has ever trusted the most meritorious real estate to its naked merits seldom does it a second time. Yet most of the "cappers" were now members of the land company making the sale or friends of the seller, who as a personal favor were allowed to bid off (or "mark off" where the sale was from the map only) a few lots to "hold for a few days" and make the advance. The few days now found prices rising so rapidly that the party for whom they were marked off generally concluded to take them for himself, and so became a genuine buyer.

In August 1887 the boom was at its height, though no one suspected it. New people were pouring in faster than ever, and jumping at everything and anything more ravenously than ever. The amount of money passing in exchange every day through the banks is so incredible to any one who has not seen the record of it that I dare not give the figures. A million was now the standard figure for a "capitalist" worthy of mention, with from three to five millions to distinguish the larger ones. "Capitalist" was now the designation of nearly every one of them, and was the common designation of a man's business in the new directories and in the letter-heads of new corporations and other places. Instead of being surprised, the majority thought it only a case of manifest destiny; and he who dared suggest any doubts about the continuance of this state of affairs was a croaker, a fossil, and what not. And the wildest of the lot were generally the new-comers from the East, who had begun to make some money out of it. They thought the old settlers fools who did not yet know the true value of their country. In general they were eminently right, though not in the sense they intended. Some of them had seen booms before. But they thought the conditions of this boom vastly different from any ever before seen. In fact this was not a boom at all, but only a sudden recognition of what the world had long been looking for and had just found. Boom? Not a bit of it. It was only a natural growth, and had only fairly started. Whether any one else had ever been stranded on the same sandbank in different conditions, they never asked. They were only certain that this was no boom, and that the conditions of its growth were something entirely new.

Nor were there many buying for speculation. Bless you, no: they were buying only for investment. The rate of interest for money in the East was a little too low. Especially does the towering genius who has made a fortune by his own exertions find five or six per cent too slow. He prides himself on being a "self-made man," and takes good care, perhaps, to tell you so; informing you often with vast superfluity that he "never had no schoolin'." Such genius cannot be content with the low interest that satisfies the born banker or the man who has inherited a stack of bonds. But of course he does not want anything too big. O no! He wants to let you know that he is a financier, by giving you the old saw that high interest and poor securities always go together. But he does want the interest to which his genius is entitled, to wit, from twelve to twenty per cent. And there is no surer way to get it than to invest in a good solidly growing town. But no speculation, for him!

And so the public sales continued from early in the morning until late in the night, with a chance for a particular friend of the seller or some capitalist of note, whose time was limited, but whose importance in the financial world deserved respect, to get in the back way on Sunday and secure a fortune on his way to church. The streets were everywhere filled with people, and the sheen of happy teeth in the sun, the everlasting blast of the brass band on the curbstone in front of the selling-places, the parading of omnibuses with big placards on the outside and a brass band within, long processions decorated with flags and headed also by the inevitable band,

and carrying with a grand flourish the lumber for the new hotel on one town-site, and the new furniture for the hotel on another, the flourish of check-books, the rushing to and fro of real-estate agents who now occupied with their offices almost every other ground floor on the business streets and in some buildings were packed like sardines in a box, the glitter of diamond rings and breast-pins, the beam of new silk hats and smiling faces all tended to steal away one's brains rather than make one more cautious. And Southern California not being large enough to hold the expected tide of humanity yet to come, and not large enough for the soaring aspirations of the investors, the boom rolled over the Mexican line into Lower California, where at various points hundreds of thousands of dollars were spent for lots at fabulous prices. And there it was the same as in California. In the hundreds of thousands of acres of fertile soil that could be bought for a song, to much of which water could be easily brought, and on much of which the subterranean water was so near the surface that for most things no irrigation was really needed, and on hundreds of thousands more where the winter rainfall is so heavy that almost anything can be raised upon it alone, scarcely any one could see any investment. But thousands of twenty-five-foot lots, some of them one hundred and seventy miles below San Diego, sold for enough, each, to buy a whole farm of fine land much nearer to market.

And yet one hardly knows whether to wonder most at such things or at the wild waste of money already secured. Thousands of people supposed to have seen something and been somewhere were acting as if money had just been discovered on this earth. A lot of savages who had raided a mint and just learned what the coin was good for, could hardly have acted worse than people fresh from the East who brought considerable money with them. Dozens of land companies in the first few days of sales sold over three hundred thousand dollars' worth of lots, of which the first payment of one third in cash was more than the whole could be worth in twenty years unless turned into fruit-land by water. And then they generally had from three-fourths to seven-eighths of the tract left. The almost uniform custom was to spend the whole of the cash for a hotel about ten times as large as could be filled in the next generation, and then anticipate the deferred payments by borrowing all that the banks would lend, to improve the tract with something else. In the counties of Los Angeles and San Bernardino the owners of these town-sites generally had sense enough to spend the money first for water for irrigation, so that the property was far from worthless. But in San Diego County water was the last thing thought of, and any extravagant nonsense for the mere convenience of future tourists took precedence. In nearly all cases there was generally debt enough incurred to swamp the whole on the least turn of the tide or any failure of the buyers to complete their payments. There were, of course, some conspicuous exceptions, such as Coronado Beach, which within one year received two and a half millions in cash, and after paying up its debts and completing all its immense improvements had four-fifths of the property left. But with four-fifths of the land companies it was the other way. One-half the money thus spent in mere convenience for future tourists if put into the development of water and railroads to open the interior and connect its different portions would have made the country the richest in the world. And one-half of the money spent for diamonds and similar stuff, if used in paying private debts would have secured a competence to hundreds who are poor to-day. But it was the old story of the beggar on horseback, except that the horse was a borrowed horse, which with a little care the rider might easily own. But no, they could not wait a few short hours. Regular "bronco busters" most of them, they had to ride the horse to death at the first dash.

A large minority kept on safe ground and are far better off to-day than they would probably ever have been if they had not played with the great boom. Some curbed their ambition to a few thousand dollars, made on a trifling investment. Others, though in some instances speculating wildly, kept carefully out of debt, and bought nothing that they could not pay for in full. Others who did not pay in full refused to give any personal obligation for the unpaid balance, and bought practically on an option with the exact amount of the risk determined. Others who were crazy enough at the beginning became suddenly scared, and concluded that it would be at least safe to "clean up."

Yet "cleaning up" was not so simple a thing as it seemed. And many a one sold out only to conclude in a few days afterward that he was a fool, and buy back perhaps some of the very property that he had sold. Mr. Jones, for instance, was a very sensible man, who had come here in 1886 with twenty thousand dollars, and had operated with good judgment and considerable caution. He now sold off half his property, and, after paying all that was due on the remainder, had over one hundred thousand dollars in bank.

Yet in less than twenty-four hours he began to feel uneasy. A dollar in a boy's pocket never burned as that money in bank did. He soon began to worry because his money was lying idle. Never having felt before the delights of idle capital, he began to soliloquize as follows:

"First thing I know, tax time will be around, and then I will either have to swear to a lie or else have it assessed at its full value, while everyone else is assessed at only one-fourth on property. In the meantime it is drawing no interest, and is not increasing in value either. If I put it in government bonds they are liable to be stolen, and if in registered bonds then they are too slow to handle in case I want to use some of it. And the interest on bonds is too low anyway. Nobody wants to borrow money now except the speculators, and I don't want to lend money to any one for that purpose. If I am going to take those chances I would just as leave take in the profit myself as see some one else do it on my money. I wonder if it is safe here in the banks if there comes a smash? And if I send it away to any of the big banks in the big cities, how do I know that it is any safer there? Some rascally cashier or president is always wrecking the best of banks everywhere. The directors put some old goat at the head of the bank because he is rich. He knows no more of what is going on inside than I do; never looks over the books, and couldn't make head or tail out of them if he looked at them every day—mere old figure-heads, all of them, that add no more to the safety of the bank than a picture of George Washington in a back-wood's gin-mill adds to the safety of the American Republic. And the bigger the figure-head and the bigger his bank the less he knows about it. Confound it, loose coin isn't such a fine thing after all. I believe real estate is the best thing to keep it in, and there is always a chance of its increasing there. I wonder, now, if I haven't been goose enough to get scared about nothing? It will certainly take at least a year to get the brakes set on such a train as this, and then it will take fully a year to slow down the train."

Mr. Smith, who had also "made a handsome killing," reasoned in much the same way, but concluded that the best way to make some more money was to hold his loose cash ready for the break and then gather in the fragments of the crockery at his own figures. Mr. Smith still makes "a handsome killing" every fall, but it is on hogs of his own raising. And they do say that the sauerkraut that Mr. Jones now puts up for market "goes first-rate" with granger Smith's pork.

Ex-granger Squizzle, who had turned his farm into a town-site, made a grand sale of lots for fifty times what they could possibly be worth in twenty years, built a seventy-five-thousand-dollar hotel, and been offered one hundred and fifty thousand dollars for his remaining interest in the whole, came also to the conclusion that it would be well to clean up. There was bound to be a collapse, he thought, and the man who had money would then be master of the situation. He had already in view several fine town-sites for the future that he would then pick up at his own figures and have ready for the next boom, which was of course going to come in about six months,

GETTING OUT. 131

or a year at the farthest, after the collapse. Of course no one else had thought of anything of the sort, and every one would be over ears in debt, and he would have all the ready cash there was. But to sell just now would be to sacrifice too much. After the Holidays would come the great rush of wealthy people, and then he would unload *so* quickly and for nearly twice what he could now! It may be incidentally remarked in passing that the very sage Mr. Squizzle now raises his own potatoes instead of buying imported ones from Humboldt County.

Other people found other difficulties.

Ex-banker Snagsby, late of Omaha (he was a Colonel now), also decided to clean up. Having been a banker, he was unusually shrewd and conservative. In a few days after deciding, he had converted two-thirds of his property into cash.

"Well, sir," said the great General Tiddlebug, meeting him on the street a few days afterward, "I told you you were throwing away that corner that you sold for fifty thousand dollars. It has just sold for fifty-five, and will bring seventy-five before Christmas."

"Got anything else to give away?" said Colonel Gote to him the next day. "I am offered fifteen per cent advance on that piece I bought of you the other day. I'll double my money on it before spring."

"I shan't kick if you make a million on it. I did well enough on it. I am cleaning up, and any man that don't do the same is a fool," replied Colonel Snagsby stiffly.

"Ye-e-e-s?" said the other colonel with a sneering rising inflection. "Permit me to return the compliment. Any man who sells anything before spring is a fool."

Ex-banker Snagsby, or rather Colonel Snagsby, had gone scarce half a block farther when Major Dinkenbat pulled him one side, and in a half whisper said:

"Say, what are you doing? Do stop this talk about cleaning up. You are injuring prices and throwing away your property too. All the boys are talking about it. You could get a good deal more by taking only one-third or a quarter cash. Talking the way you do and selling for cash only, you hurt the market."

"I am going to sit down for awhile on a little cold coin. You may yet find it a comfortable thing to sit on, yourself."

The Major looked at him a moment with pitying air, and said:

"I wouldn't swap what I've got in this town for a chunk of solid gold twenty feet square, with the whole United States army and forty bulldogs to guard it for me."

Two years later the Colonel happened to dine with the Major on his homestead claim in the mountains. The Colonel said he did not eat beans, so the Major told him to help himself to the mustard.

"I wonder now if I haven't been a trifle too fast," said the Colonel this time, as he left the Major. "I guess not, though. It is better to be safe than to take the chances on making more." This is the way many conservative bankers reason when there is no chance to make anything. It is very easy to be conservative when there is no boom. "When the sea is calm, all boats alike show mastership in floating." While thus formulating abstract principles that may govern the average conservative banker in common times, he strolled into the affectionate embrace of a little near-sighted chap who poked his nose in his face and sputtered out as fast as he could rattle.

"Know that piece 'longside the one you sold

the other day on Mackerel Street? Get it for you for fifty thousand. Only quarter cash. Divvy commish with you. Seventy thousand refused yesterday for the piece you sold 'longside of it. Biggest buy in town."

"Confound it. I knew I ought to have held that a while longer. Well, let it go. There is nothing like being safe," said Snagsby, as he walked on.

A singular feature of such times is how so many who are in the whirl, amid all the rush and bustle, know one another's movements—what each one is buying, what he is offering, what he is refusing, and what he thinks of the situation. So it was not strange that when Snagsby came down the street the next morning, Judge Snapper, another millionaire, should ask him:

"Is it possible that you sold that corner on Banana Street for twenty thousand? I told some one it could not be so."

The ex-banker was about to say yes, but a sudden feeling of shame overtook him. In his mind's eye he saw a man deliberately throwing away five or ten thousand dollars. And the situation was not at all relieved by seeing Judge Snapper eying him from foot to foot, as who should say, "What manner of man is this, anyway?"

"I believe I did sell that a little too cheap. I wish I had it back," said Snagsby to himself as he walked on.

"Been looking for you all over," said a man rushing up to him an hour later. "Got a most exquisite snap for you. Not another such bargain on the planet. Only fifteen hundred a foot for a corner on northwest of Pineapple and Orange.

"Don't want it. I have quit buying."

"Q-u-i-t b-u-y-i-n-g?" said the man with eyes expanded in astonishment, and stepping back a pace or two to survey the Colonel from head to foot more thoroughly than the Judge had just done. "Q-u-i-t b-u-y-i-n-g? May I be eternally scorched if that isn't strange talk. Why, it is the very time of all times to commence."

"Don't want it," said Snagsby savagely, as he moved on.

"I say," he added, turning around before he had gone five steps farther, "half cash will fetch that considerably cheaper, won't it?"

"W-e-l-l n-o-w, it—might be shaded a trifle, I suppose, when I come to think about it. The fact is, the owner's wife is whining to get back East to her mammy. He thinks the world of her, and might sacrifice a little to please her," said the man after some meditation.

"Well, I don't believe I want it," said Snagsby, turning around to go.

But before he had taken three steps he wheeled half around again, and said, "By the way, what will all cash take it in for?"

"O—h! W-e-l-l n-o-w, that makes a difference. The price might be shaded a bit for cash."

"You can throw off the commission too, can't you?"

"W-e-l-l n-o-w. That's asking too much. I—ah—might divvy with you, though, to make a trade."

"Well, I ain't particularly stuck on it any how," said Snagsby, walking off, vowing that he would buy nothing more at any price. But he could not resist the temptation to see the man the same afternoon, and play around the subject just to see how cheap he could get it. It was in truth a fine piece of property, and was well worth the price asked for it—that is, it would be when the town had five or six times the population it then had. During the night he allowed his fancy to play over it, and several times he imagined it was his.

And before the next sun rode the western slope of blue it was his.

And thus one after another, dozens of those who had swum ashore and shaken the water off were drawn again into the vortex. The temptation was one that no man can tell whether he can stand until he tries it. The more one examined the situation the more ridiculous it seemed to be content with a few thousand, when at one swoop one could just as well make a fortune. To tell any one that ten thousand was a fortune for the average mortal, and that the chance to make it out of nothing in a year was one that does not occur to one out of a thousand in a lifetime, was only to insult him. Even to one who never before had fifty dollars ahead in the world, ten thousand seemed pitiably contemptible now. He heard rich and successful men say every day that this boom was different from all others, that it had such different conditions that it could never stop, that it almost took away one's breath to think of the danger one had run in even thinking of selling before the grand rush of the Universe set in.

Nor was it such an easy matter to swim out of the main current and keep near shore. Hundreds thought of it and turned their heads that way, but when it came to making even the first bold stroke they weakened and drifted back into the whirl again.

Mr. Sniffins, for instance, was a good lawyer in good practice, and a man of far more than ordinary shrewdness. He had invested in real estate all the profits of his business, and all the money he could borrow of the banks. On the basis on which all such estimates were now made he was worth half a million, and he could have sold out in forty-eight hours for two hundred thousand dollars in money. Of course the whole country could not have sold out for any such proportion of people's estimated wealth, for there was not money enough in circulation west of the Mississippi to have paid for it all. But any one person could in almost one day have sold for one-third or two-fifths of his estimated wealth. And almost all those who were in debt could in the summer of 1887 have sold enough to have cleared the rest of their holdings.

Lawyer Sniffins felt that he had a fortune assured, and ought to put it beyond the reach of disagreeable possibilities. His calculations on the future might be mistaken. At the same time it was the last time in the world to make a mistake.

Such chances to get rich on nothing rarely strike any one in a lifetime, and one must be careful about throwing them away. It is strange that while so many reasoned in this way, few could see that the fact that such opportunities are so rare is the very reason why one should make sure of a moderate sum. And many do reason in this way. The trouble is to know in a boom what a moderate sum is. Lawyer Sniffins reasoned so. But to him half a million now looked very moderate among so many millionaires, most of whom had made their whole fortune in a year or eighteen months when nothing looked half as brilliant as everything now looked. In these days, when it takes so much more money to make a man than it used to take, it is no trifling matter to throw away a quarter of a million by a little timidity. There was so much doubt in the mind of Sniffins that he concluded to consult some of the leading bankers and other wise men of the town, for he had now been rich long enough to appreciate the wisdom of other rich men, which he never could do when poor.

He strolled into one of the leading banks and was met with a beamy smile by the head of the bank. The banker rubbed his hand affectionately between his own hands, and inquired with deep tenderness of tone after the health of his very good wife and family; for Mr. Sniffins' deposits, though not distressingly large, showed a very steady balance, and when he wanted money he borrowed it at good interest, and never troubled the bank with overdrafts.

"What do you think of the situation? How long is it going to last? I am thinking of cleaning up so as to be on the safe side," said Mr. Sniffins.

"Well," said the banker, with the ponderous gravity of utterance becoming the wisdom of wealth, "I can't fully agree with those who think it is going to last forever. But I am satisfied that the top is still a long way off. I am holding everything I have, and I see no special cause for doing otherwise. Of course I would not advise any one to buy what he cannot pay for; but I see no reason for sacrificing anything, and to sell before winter is certainly to sacrifice some."

This bit of wisdom was cut suddenly short by the arrival of two Eastern capitalists, who came in to consult the banker about investments. They represented a class of capitalists unusually shrewd. The majority of them could hardly wait to eat before buying something. But a shrewd minority always consulted a leading banker before buying, thinking that a successful banker knows all about Southern California, when in fact his knowledge of the land and the true basis of its prosperity is generally in inverse proportion to the magnitude of his bank.

The next banker Mr. Sniffins called on, like the last one, meant to be honest in his opinions, but as he was himself speculating he did not want the market broken by too much " cleaning up." Sniffins did not deposit in this bank, but the banker considering the possibility of his doing so some day, allowed a peach-and-creamy smile to develop itself.

"Money has never before come in so fast as it is coming now," said the banker, rubbing his own hands and quite forgetting about the health of Lawyer Sniffins' family. "We are now building new vaults to hold our increasing deposits," he continued, giving Lawyer S. to understand that his patronage was not essential to the success of the bank. "I have made two millions in the last two years and am making it now faster than ever."

"How much of it have you in cash?" inquired the lawyer.

"O, I keep very little of it in cash, of course. Money doesn't increase in value like property."

"Don't you think it would be well to hang up a slice where the cats can't get at it?"

"Certainly, certainly; but it isn't time yet. I expect to clean up and get everything ready for a big smash. But you see the winter travel hasn't even begun yet. About February there will be an amount of people and money here that will eclipse everything we have yet seen."

As Lawyer Sniffins went out he met on the corner, arrayed in spotless garb, with teeth shining in a chronic smile that almost dimmed the sparkle of his diamond ring and breastpin, one of the great millionaires of the town—General Nubbins. Before the boom he was only plain "Cap" Nubbins, and nobody asked his opinion on anything connected with making money, though he was a fair judge of the weight of a steer. But now Sniffins could not resist the temptation to ask him whether he were buying or selling.

The picturesque face of the General changed on the instant. A cloud of indignant surprise overspread the smiling landscape.

"Buying, Sir, of course," he said, stepping back a pace or two and surveying the rash mortal who had asked the question. "It is *madness* to sell anything now—*stark madness*, sir." And taking hold of the lappels of his coat and drumming on his breast with his fingers he leaned back upon one leg, an imposing monument of wisdom.

Even after one had firmly resolved to sell, it was no easy matter to keep the resolution. Dr. Podly, for instance, had been back East for a few weeks closing up some old business and found that all the papers were now abusing California, sneering at the boom, advising people to keep away, and publishing all manner of absurd stuff from disappointed parties who had been ill-treated at some overcrowded hotel, or overcharged at some lodging-house, or who found that their little hoard would not buy within the limits of some established city a farm that could be at once cut into thousand-dollar lots. The doctor saw abundant evidence of a coming reaction and hurried back, intending to sell at once. But when he went upon the street and saw how the town had grown in his short absence, how everything was selling faster and at higher prices than ever, he hesitated. That very day the first Pullman excursion of the season arrived, and discharged upon the crazy town several car-loads of "first-class travel,"—" first-class travel," meaning more money and airs with no more brains than ordinary travel. The "first-class" soon mingled with the crowd, rushing here and there to buy, and the richer any one of them appeared, the more crazy he seemed. A new town-site thrown on the market this day with the express purpose of catching this crowd made a finer catch of gudgeons than anything yet offered, and the "first-class" jumped at the bare hook in such reckless manner that it set the fishermen themselves more crazy than ever. Another excursion was due in two weeks, and such excursions were to run all winter. The temptation to make a few dollars more simply by waiting a few days was too strong for the doctor. He saw the danger clearly enough, and resolved to escape it. But next week would surely be time enough, and when next week came it seemed so easy to get more by waiting a few days that he could not resist the temptation to let prices rise just a little bit higher.

CHAPTER IX.

THE COLLAPSE.

LIKE a thief in the night the decline came on. None suspected the day of its coming less than those whose experience in other booms told them precisely where the top of this one was, or those who knew that all other booms were very uncertain, but saw entirely different conditions in this one.

"Isn't it a trifle dull this week?" said Major Peach the first week in January, 1888, to General Snoodle, the owner of Wildcat Park. The General twirled his long goatee several times around his two fingers, and after a few moments' meditation replied:

"Well, you know it is always so about the Holidays. By the way, I feel a trifle dry. What do you say to a cocktail?"

"Seems to me sales are not quite as lively as they were," remarked Judge Dumble to another "Judge."

"P-o-s-s-i-b-l-y n-o-t," replied Judge number two with a French shrug that tumbled the ashes of a twenty-five-cent cigar down his shirt bosom. "This is Presidential year, you know, and business is always a little dull in such years. It strikes me, however, that it is a mighty long time between drinks this morning. I have never been so dry in my life. I believe it is this cussed east wind."

Whereupon they locked arms and disappeared through a gilded doorway.

"*S-a-y!* isn't it a *l-e-e-t-l-e* mite quiet?" said Colonel Foodle in a hoarse whisper to General Billick, the enterprising proprietor of Badger Heights.

"Well—you—know—it is always a little slow at this time of the year," said the General, pulling the tip of his nose meditatively with his thumb and forefinger, and looking furtively around to see that there were no strangers within hearing. "The payment of taxes, you know, about Christmas takes a lot of money out of circulation. By the way, isn't it about eleven o'clock? Somehow I feel extra dry this morning."

"Seems to me it's letting up a bit," said Commodore Stubbins to General Sneezer, the proprietor of Coyote Vista.

"Why, of course," said the General, seeing some strangers approaching. "Do you suppose anybody is fool enough to sell now? Ahem! I feel mighty dry this morning. I believe it's this blasted east wind. I am holding on to everything I have. Ahem! Suppose we go over the way and irrigate a bit."

"It looks as if it were closing down. We have neglected all true development and run prices out of all reason. We have killed the goose that laid the golden egg, and will have to stand the consequences," said the very plain Mr. Grey to the prince of the millionaires, General Gumpey.

"Prices—too—*high?*" spluttered out the General from the midst of an orange in which he was delving. His face grew red, and with gray eyes bulging with wrath he glared at the audacious mortal known as Grey. "Prices—too—*high?*" he exclaimed again as soon as he could catch the breath he had lost in astonishment and indignation. "Such talk as that, Sir, would bust a boom in the New Jerusalem. If there is anything the matter it is the talk of folks like you, always talking about back country and water, and making fools believe that such things are necessary. But thank Gawd, Sir, you can't damage this bay or this climate. There is nothing the matter, Sir, except that a lot of fools have quit throwing away their property, and are holding it for decent figures."

"*I* think she's busted," interposed a roughly dressed man who stood by listening.

"We can dispense with commentators, Sir," said the General, grandly.

"You dig me up and you'll find me a mighty uncommon tater," said the man, bristling up to the General. "I blowed in a year's wages on your town-site, and I'd like to see some returns from it."

"The deuce," replied the General with creamy smile. "Why, you must be one of the very chaps I've been looking for. My agent disobeyed my orders, and sold some of those lots too cheap, and I have been trying to find the buyers so as to buy it back. Let's go over the way and take a smile first, and then we'll see about it."

"I am afraid the thing is shutting down," said Judge Dumpling to the Rev. Solomon Sunrise.

"Have no fears, my dear Sir," said the Rev. Solomon, laying his hand on the other's shoulder, while a kind smile suffused his thoughtful features. "This is only a shadow cast by the lesser light in the presence of the greater. What we have hitherto thought the full blaze of prosperity was but a tallow-candle that now casts a shadow under the light of the great rising sun of the immediate future. Life, Sir, is but a cobweb that the broom of death may sweep down at any moment; but our glorious climate, like the eternal smile of Heav—"

"Say," interrupted Major Snooks, pulling him suddenly to one side, "I have concluded to take that offer you made me on that lot the other day."

A dismal blank at once took the place of the late hopeful smile.

"I—I—ah—didn't—ah—suppose—that you—would take it, and ah—have made other disposition of my funds," replied the Rev. Solomon.

"Well, what will you give for it?"

"I—I don't feel quite prepared to—ah—invest this morning. In fact, I haven't time. I have to go now to prepare my discourse for the coming Sabbath."

"Well, make me an offer on it. You wanted it pretty bad the other day, and it is the best buy in town. My wife is making a big fuss about being so far away from her friends, and I'll have to take her back, I suppose, to please her. I'll have to do it even at a big sacrifice, or there'll be no peace in the house. What will you give now?"

"I—I really am not prepared to invest just now in anything, and haven't time this morning. I must go to my study at once." Whereupon the Rev. Solomon Sunrise vanished around the corner, leaving the other man smelling a very large-sized rat. He had thought he was the only one who had found out that anything was the matter, and had expected to unload on the unsophisticated parson.

For several days the numerous generals, colonels, majors, judges, doctors, and professors (strange to say, there were no admirals, and only one commodore was to be found) whom boom-money had evolved from very common clay, talked over matters on the streets and in the gilded bar-rooms, whither an almost universal aridity of the throat had driven them. And the opinion was quite universal that prospects were really brighter than before, and that the elements of success were only preparing for a greater storm than ever yet was dreamed of.

Nevertheless something was the matter, for "the boys" who had been drinking for dinner French champagne at four dollars a bottle, or rather California champagne at double the price for a French label, to which they had gradually ascended from bottled beer in a chromatic scale, which formed a perfect boom-thermometer, now made an alarming drop to California Champagne under its own name, instead of paying two dollars more for a French label.

"I tell you there is something the matter," said Professor Snipkins to Captain Popsure; "what do you think it is?"

"Damfino," replied the Captain abstractedly.

"Have there been any sales lately?"

"Damfino."

"I am afraid it's over, ain't you?"

"Damfino."

"Our only salvation is to stand by our prices. If we waver on them we are gone. Don't you think so?"

"Damfino."

In about a week more the whole of Southern California was in about the same state of mind as the Captain. Eastern people were still coming as fast as ever, and the excursion trains and hotels were all crowded. But there was a weird stillness in the real-estate market, and "the boys" made an alarming drop from Champagne to Riesling without tarrying even a day at the half-way house of Sauterne. It was now conceded by the wise—the wise meaning those only who had made some money on the boom—that there was a lull. But the wise also decided that it was only temporary, and that real estate would move in the spring. Meanwhile they found deep satisfaction in blaming the impending Presidential election, the tax collector, the croakers, and everything except the monstrous rents, absurd prices, the neglect of nearly all true development in the greater part of the land, and the enormous waste in every form of nonsense of money that should have been used in paying debts and developing latent resources.

The money market tightened almost on the instant.

From every quarter of the land the drain of money outward had been enormous, and had been balanced only by the immense amount constantly coming in. Almost from the day this inflow ceased money seemed scarce everywhere, for the outgo still continued. Not only were vast sums going out every day for water-pipe, railroad-iron, cement, lumber and other material for the great improvements going on in every direction, most of which material had already been ordered, but thousands more were still going out for diamonds and a thousand other things already bought—things that only increase the general indebtedness of a community by making those who cannot afford them try to imitate those who can. And tens of thousands more were going out for butter, eggs, pork, and even potatoes and other vegetables which the luxurious boomers thought it beneath the dignity of millionaires to raise. If ever a country was thoroughly prepared for a complete paralysis for ten or fifteen years it was this country. That it has passed through the decline as it has without a bank or well-established business house or legitimate business enterprise failing, and is prospering as it is to-day in spite of all the folly, is the most astonishing fact in its whole history.

CHAPTER X.

THE OVERLOADED.

It is difficult to say which is the more remarkable—the ease with which one in such a boom can imagine one's self worth a quarter of a million made out of almost nothing, or the ease with which the same person can convince himself that he is not mistaken about the solidity of his fortune. The more his better judgment questions it, and the more he debates the subject with himself, the stronger his morbid judgment becomes. The standard of values to which his mind has unconsciously grown during the excitement becomes for a time permanent, and he cannot ignore it even if he would. Consequently it is not strange that the number of those who at first saw anything alarming in the situation was very small. But it was strange that those who felt the least alarm were generally those who knew nothing of the solid foundation on which the land rested. Had they been correct in their ideas that it was going to be a great country anyhow without regard to resources, a country needing nothing but beauty, comfort, and climate to build it up, the ruin that would have followed would have had no parallel on earth. But it was their good fortune to be mistaken, and thousands were saved from beggary in spite of themselves.

Nevertheless there were many who took the alarm and resolved to sell. But there seemed no special haste about it. One could of course sell at any time at a sacrifice if necessary, and there was no use in doing so until it was necessary. But General Applehead, who had some two millions worth of property scattered about in various towns, upon which he owed a little matter of some two hundred thousand dollars, awoke one morning soon after the lull and concluded that that little two hundred thousand might not be such a bagatelle as he had so far considered it. By the time he had finished dressing he concluded that he would at once sell off enough to pay his debts, at any rate. He was not at all afraid of the rest, but thought it might be well to pay off everything.

He at once put some of his best property on the market. Before he realized it two weeks were lost in discovering that it would not sell for the same price he had been offered for it only three weeks before.

He at once became alarmed, and said to the agent, "Sell it for five thousand less, then."

"What the jewee do you want to do that faw?" said the agent, an ex-broker from the East, who had made considerable here on the boom. "Do you want to ruin the mahket entiahly?"

"Hang the market. Do as I tell you, and be mighty spry about it, too," said the General.

"All right," said the agent, and lost two weeks more in trying to sell it for the old price so as to pocket the difference. The next month was lost in trying several other agents with about the same results, and the General finally concluded that he would have to take the field himself. He was no mean hand at selling real estate for other people, but knew too well that it is often unwise to try to sell for yourself. But now he felt compelled to do so, and hunted up a rich old chap from St. Paul who a few weeks before had made him a large offer for some of his property. But the old gentleman sucked wisdom from the head of his cane, and stared at him over his glasses with a frosty eye that blighted the General's hopes at once—a stare so strangely different from the eager beam that lately lit up the eye of the capitalist while trying to buy something for fifty times what it was worth, that the General felt alarmed. The different shades of wisdom that illumine the face of the capitalist during a boom and after one would make a great subject for a painter. No, excuse me—I am wrong again, for no one could be persuaded that it was the same face.

Wherever the General had anything to sell he found the same difficulty. Everywhere was now the smile of supreme wisdom mingled with contempt for everything in California. Nor was this limited to the trash over which they had gone crazy a few weeks before, but with the great majority of strangers, who were still as numerous as ever, it was for everything in the land. The General got a few nibbles at greatly reduced prices, but the fish were so tender in the mouth that it was impossible to land them. After about two months of hard work he found himself in the position of the hunter who was willing to let go of the bear at a very reasonable discount on his expectations.

"Confound the plagued stuff! how it sticks to my fingers! It's harder to let go of than redhot pitch," said the General to himself one evening after a hard day's work. "But I must sell something mighty soon, for the banks are howling for their money, and when a banker wants his money in such times he wants it mighty bad."

For nearly a week he wandered around half dazed. The idea that with so much property he could not raise money enough to pay off the lightest of his obligations was something appalling to a man who had never before seen the time when he could not pay all his debts in twenty-four hours. Nor did he find much consolation in the fact that a large majority of the late millionaires were being appalled in the same way. They had all now discovered that pay-day is the swiftest anniversary in the year; but not even yet had they discovered that real estate is the slowest of all commodities to handle at anything near its supposed value on a dead market. They had deemed it the safest of all investments because it cannot run away, forgetting that it is safe only for those who can afford to hold it through long periods of decline. Forgetting that it is the easiest of all things with which to drug the market, people are slow to realize the fact of its depreciation. The knowledge is generally acquired at the bottom of the ladder, and just a trifle too late to utilize.

Most of the overloaded ones thought at first they were making great concessions in reducing prices ten or fifteen per cent. By the time they learned that this reduction was not enough it was too late to reduce it twenty-five per cent; and by the time they discovered this, even forty or fifty would not have effected sales enough to save them. An immediate slaughter of fondest expectations would undoubtedly have saved many, and left them still richer than they had any right to expect on the amount invested. But it could not have saved the majority. A wholesale break of prices to even one fourth of what they had been for the very best property would have inspired the buyers only with contempt, and made them believe that by waiting a little longer they could get it for next to nothing. For the vast majority of the moneyed strangers that were still coming knew nothing of the sustaining power of the land, and thought that everything stood on the same basis as the wild-cat town-lots.

And again the blaze of color burned out along

the plains and slopes, somber tints robed hill and dale, and the long, bright summer of 1888 came on.

"She has struck bottom," said some.

And in truth there was some ground for this belief, for "the boys" were drinking water again for dinner, having made a sudden descent without tarrying a day on claret either with or without a French label, and stopping only a week on bottled beer. But the end was not yet.

Times became gradually duller, and those who were making the most desperate efforts to sell anything at what seemed any price within reason were generally a trifle behind the steady lowering of prices, which were falling almost everywhere in spite of the determination of people to hold them up. The slightest rise in the temperature of the seller was followed at once by a corresponding reduction in the pulse of the buyer, and a sale of anything but productive land outside the towns was next to impossible. A few succeeded in selling lots or dry land at greatly reduced prices, but the number of sales was so slight compared with the number of the overloaded that they were little relief to the general situation.

He who tried to find encouragement among the real-estate agents often fared as Major Stumpkins did one morning when he went the rounds to see if there were any prospects of a sale having been made of any of the property he had given them. The first agent was gazing idly at the vacant doorway of his lately busy office.

"Well," said the Major, "how is real estate to-day?"

"A little easier this morning, thank you," replied the agent.

The Major came very near asking him which way, but caught himself in time.

"Any nibbles to-day?" he asked of the next one.

"Bushels of them. But they are all on the pole end of the tackle," was the answer.

In the next office he found the occupant, a late millionaire, thumbing over his "property book." There was such deep sadness on the man's face as he looked at the huge figures in the right-hand column, reflected on the glorious past, and thought of what the lots would now bring, that the Major did not trouble him.

The next one he found in his office figuring carefully over the stubs in his check-book to see whether it would be safe to draw a check for five dollars to keep his gas from being cut off that day.

Another late millionaire he found fumbling over with melancholy satisfaction his returned bank checks of the preceding year. He was thinking of the champagne and other good things he had enjoyed, and, rich in the memory of the past, he smiled grimly at fate, little imagining that before another year he was doomed to wring his bread from the soil in the "back country" that in his ignorant pride he had never seen or even cared to see.

"Any sign of things picking up?" inquired the Major of another who stood leaning against a lamp-post in front of his office with hands up to the elbows in his empty pockets.

"O yes. About a couple of dozen families picked up yesterday and lit out," said the man without looking up.

Of course the news now went abroad that the boom was "busted" and the bottom was "clean out." Even the ancient simile of the rats and the sinking ship was dragged out and made to do full duty far and wide throughout the North and East. And it was in a measure applicable. Some of the rats were deserting the ship; and it was equally true that the said rats were now doing about all the newspaper correspondence, and were apparently the only correspondents now desired by the press of certain sections.

A grand and everlasting crash had been generally predicted for San Diego. That it did not happen, its people may thank, not themselves, but that kind Providence that watches over children and fools, and that, with not one in a hundred either caring or knowing anything about it, put a prosperous population in the country behind it larger that of the city itself. It is a hard thing perhaps to say of one's home, and especially of a home where one has as many good friends as the writer has in San Diego, but if ever a people deserved utter ruin for ignoring and despising great and valuable resources, it is the people who have made San Diego the city that it is to-day. For years it had been almost universally said of San Diego, that it had "no back country and no water." Such was the common belief throughout the whole of the coast above it and the United States generally wherever its name was known. From the north southward, every part of California has in its turn been deemed a desert, fit only for cattle ranges. As each county has in turn emerged from the desert state, it has turned out a fairer and richer garden than the last place that had been found not to be a desert. Yet each newly discovered garden in its turn forgot that it had once been a desert, and never contemplated the possibility of being mistaken in the same old way about the next county on the south of it. At the beginning of the boom San Diego County was the last link in the chain of deserts, and occupied the same place in public opinion that the rich and beautiful counties of San Bernardino, Los Angeles, and Orange had held ten years before. With a vast expanse of beautiful country and a perfect climate for the raising of the most valuable products, with a million acres of as fertile soil as any of the fruit-growing sections of the State, with an abundant rainfall in its mountains and a greater number of fine reservoir sites for the making of great lakes than almost any other county in the state, it was almost as unknown to the world at large as the wilds of Alaska. Most of its arable lands are broken up into tracts of a few thousand acres each, and these tracts are hidden one from another by low dividing ridges, every one of which seems at first to be the end of all the good land there is. And the whole is hidden still more from the common lines of travel by the broken edge of the immense table-land that stretches some seventy miles along its coast and reaches some ten miles back. This table-land, though nearly all rich soil and the largest body of arable land in the United States that is generally free from frost, was almost uninhabited because of the depth of the water in the wells. Like Riverside, Redlands, Pasadena, and others of the finest parts of California, it had to lie a desert until water could be brought upon it from the mountains. But the scholars and statesmen, and sages and capitalists, and newspaper men and professional tourists, took but one look at its ragged outer edge where it breaks off to the sea-coast, and at once passed full and final judgment upon a county larger than the State in which many of them were born.

One half the people who have built the handsome buildings and made the great improvements in San Diego fully believed this old-time story, while three fourths of the rest neither knew nor cared whether it were true or not. Thousands of people had looked at the city and its bay, and said: " Your bay is perfect, your climate is beyond doubt the finest on earth; but if this is all you have, I don't want any of it."

Yet they neither heard nor heeded such common-sense talk. Worshiping their bay and climate with a blind idolatry, they really believed that these two alone would build up a great city on the edge of a desert with only water enough to wash in and dilute whisky with, and with no exports but sand, money, and empty beer barrels. Ask any citizen during the boom whether San Diego had any back country, and the answer was quite certain to be—

"Why, certainly, the whole United States is our back country."

"But have you nothing a little nearer?"

"Why, of course, there is the whole of Arizona and New Mexico."

"But I mean something more immediate."

"Certainly, certainly! We have the whole of Southern California."

"But I mean something close by, where one can raise something."

"Raise something? Why, it don't matter, my dear Sir, if you can't raise a bean within fifty miles of this bay."

The reader will hardly believe me when I say

that during the boom there were maps of the United States in several of the real-estate offices, with the words "San Diego's back country" pasted over the top in large letters. Once in a while the visitor met a man with sense enough to see the folly of such talk as the above, and who stoutly declared that there was a fine back country. But when it came to telling anything about it, or where it was, or how to see it, he often showed conclusively that he knew nothing about it before he had had his mouth open two minutes.

CHAPTER XI.

TURNING OVER A NEW LEAF.

THE people of Southern California excelled the world in the quickness with which they turned over a new leaf as much as they excelled it in blotting the old one with folly. At the first symptom of decline, and before people in the cities had discovered anything serious, the people in the country went to work as never before. Not a moment did they lose in mourning over their shattered idols or whining around the grave of empty hopes. Everywhere the plow was aroused from its two years' sleep, and the cackle of the hen was heard on many a lovely town-site. Neglected orchards were put in the best of order, and town-lot stakes pulled up from hundreds of grass-grown fields. The brush was cleared from a thousand hill-sides that had never felt the plow, and by the first of May 1888 the area of cultivated land was nearly fifty per cent larger than it had ever been.

And yet the general indebtedness weighed down the whole country and made hard times in the midst of what was really high prosperity. For in spite of the collapse in the speculative bubble new people were coming, and outside of the towns were buying and settling as fast as ever. In some places the settlement was actually more rapid than it had been during the height of the boom, because those who came with the intention of cultivating the soil now went out to look at some of it, instead of trying to double their money on town-lots first.

But nearly all buying except for actual use had ceased, and those who wanted land for use could get it at very nearly their own figures. All except the irrigated land; which being cheap as a plain business investment at the highest price ever asked for it, and never having had a boom, had not only not fallen in selling value, but in some places, as at Highlands, Redlands, and East Riverside, sold higher and faster than ever. But fully two thirds of the speculators were overloaded with dry land and town-lots. With a thousand times more real estate on the market than was necessary to supply the demands of legitimate business, and nearly every one crazy to sell, but still fondly imagining that the old values were nearly correct, one can imagine the difficulties of any one entangled in a net of debt, with a load of unproductive property for his only assets. Vainly the real-estate agents posted their bulletin-boards with long lists of town property, with the word "snaps" at the head. Even the common addition of the word "soft" did not help the matter. People now were not looking for "soft snaps," but for something that did not depend for its value on the chances of selling to some one else in sixty days.

And so the summer of 1888 passed away. There was in the cities a distressing amount of *statu quo*, and the state of affairs grew rapidly no better. Though the towns were everywhere losing their floating population brought in by the boom, the number of inhabitants to the dollar was still painfully too great. Could our economic writers have studied these times, they could have learned that something besides taxes and tariffs and a single-standard of money may cause distress. It is possible that the steady increase of general indebtedness, caused by extravagance and the anxiety to get rich enough to ape other rich people, is a far greater factor than is commonly supposed.

Yet before winter came it was evident that there would be no such crash as would naturally be expected in the reaction from such long-continued folly, waste, and extravagance. Even before the next summer was spent it was noticed that money was no scarcer than in the winter shortly after the decline began. In some mysterious way the immense amount still going daily out was being replaced. The sneering wise men who came from the North and East to laugh at the wreck or gather up the fragments at their own price stood agape with wonder when they found that no property was put under the hammer to sell for what it would bring in cash; that almost every improvement begun during the boom was being finished; that new houses and stores better than any yet built were rising in all the larger cities and established centers of business; and, above all, that outside of the towns the whole country was filling with new settlers more rapidly than ever.

Those only could explain this who for years had watched the growth of Southern California, and knew the basis on which it rested. A few of these had all along predicted that there would be no "grand smash," but only a steady settling to the business foundation on which people should have kept the boom—the foundation on which it started. And so it turned out. Although the crowding and jostling at the real-estate offices were gone, people had by no means stopped coming to Southern California. Only the speculators and old grannies, who are afraid to buy anything on their own judgment and have to wait for leaders, were scared.

Nor were people leaving to any great extent. Much of the floating population necessarily went away because it should never have come. But of the many who left the cities fully one half sought the country, and made their first acquaintance with Mother Earth. Many more should have gone, but remained in the towns awaiting the return of the boom, and adding by their gloomy looks to the general depression.

However empty may have been the apparent basis seen only by the superficial glance of the tourist or crazy speculator, an excitement lasting so long, extending over so great an area of both town and country, and bringing in so large a proportion of wealthy and permanent settlers, must have had a solid foundation. Behind all the nonsense lay the great productive power of the soil.

Though too many ignored or forgot this, it was steadily having its effect. Though too many had neglected their land or spoiled it with town-lot stakes, and too many were buying from others what they could raise even better themselves, the amount of produce was still very great. The last year of the boom, Riverside alone, from only four thousand acres of land actually producing, received a million of dollars from its trees and vines. The receipts of other sections for fruit—fresh, canned, and dried, though not so easy to ascertain as those of Riverside, were still enormous for the acreage; while the money received from grain, honey, wool, nuts, beans, mines, and other things mounted into the millions. San Diego County itself, although almost unknown, was receiving from different products nearly a million a year.

Even for those who as yet made only a living from the soil, the difference between the sustaining power of the land here and at their old homes was very great. The difference in the cost of going through the winter, and in the cost of house and barn, and a dozen other things in this mild climate, enabled one even on the unirrigated lands to hold one's farm and support a family under circumstances that would have made it impossible in any Eastern State. On the irrigated tracts the making of a good living on only ten acres, since the discovery of the proper methods of irrigation and cultivation, was now so easy for the laziest man, and for the industrious man the making of a fine profit above the living was now so certain since the markets of the world were buying all the California fruit they could get, that a man, once settled on such a place, could not be driven from it by any pressure of the times.

"Booms are detrimental," said the Reverend Solomon Sunrise one day, when, after long cogitation over vain efforts to sell something, he had come to the conclusion that he was not as rich as he thought he was.

"You're right," replied Major Dinkenbat. "But all the same I would like a whack at another one for about forty-eight hours."

The Reverend Solomon was right this time. The boom delayed the development of those resources in which that country excels all other lands, and which will yet give it its greatest prosperity. Though in a few places like San Bernardino County and a part of Los Angeles County they were sensible enough to put the strangers' money into water-works and other solid improvements, in the greater part of the country it was squandered with shameful waste. Nevertheless the boom strung the land with railroad iron, cement sidewalks, street-railroads, sewers, gas-pipes, electric wires, and other valuable and permanent improvements. Everywhere, amid the evidences of waste and folly rose solidity that with the common pace of progress could not have come in years. It added also a permanent population of over a hundred thousand people, all of whom have now settled down to honest work.

Meanwhile there was no such crackling of bones as Eastern and Northern papers had predicted, or as would have been heard in an old and crystallized community. A few creditors were merciless, and refused to take back at any price property on which they had received a one-third payment, which was more than the whole could possibly be worth in the next ten years. But the great majority knew how it was themselves, and, looking at the whole fabric of society as a row of bricks on end, were disposed to do what was fair. Consequently liquidation began almost from the first month of the decline, and dozens were every day released from their obligations. Some received a part of what they had bought equal to the payment they had made, and got a release for the remainder of the debt. Others were released from the whole of it by deeding back the property and losing what they had paid on it. Some exchanged other property for the unpaid balance, while some had the balance remitted in consideration of improving the land. In many cases there was no personal obligation to pay any more than the sum already paid, and the whole contract amounted only to an option on the part of the buyer.

Nevertheless the number of lame ducks and of those who had no legitimate business, but were merely hanging around waiting for the boom to begin again (a thing in which nearly all had the utmost confidence), was still so great that the times were hard in the midst of real prosperity.

CHAPTER XII.

THE FALLING OF THE ROSES.

AGAIN from the top of the great dome of blue the clarion tones of the sand-hill crane echoed to the tender pipe of the little plover trotting over the greensward below, the curlew were spinning in bands along the shore, and the snowy form of the egret shone again in the bright sun along the inlets and lagoons; flocks of teal went whizzing through the night, sea-birds circled around the dark rotunda that enclosed the top of the electric-light masts, and the winter of 1888–9 came on with nearly every one expecting a grand catch of "tenderfeet," because the elections were over and Florida had had the yellow-fever. The stranger came in fair numbers, spent a little money at hotels, barber-shops, and saloons, and as usual went away without seeing anything of California. For the great increase of grain-fields, vineyards, orchards and vegetable gardens he had no eye. That not a bank or large business house or legitimate enterprise of any kind had failed, and that outside the cities the land was growing with a more substantial growth than ever, he never discovered. Nearly all his faculties were concentrated on some town-lot stakes that some goose had put in and had not yet sense enough to pull up.

The great American capitalist was on hand too in considerable force. And oh, how smart! He wouldn't have bought anything the year before— not he. He knew all about it now. As usual, he took a stroll around a few blocks in San Diego, and decided that it had no "back country." He basked on the porches of the monster hotel at Coronado, and revised his opinion only to become more firmly convinced that his opinion was infallible. Nevertheless over twenty thousand people were already living where back of the city he saw only dreamy hills, the plow was subduing a hundred thousand acres more than ever before, thousands of acres of new vineyard and orchard were planting, and new people were settling every day. Even in the counties adjoining, where the country tributary to the cities is as easy to see as in San Diego County it is difficult to see, the tourist saw little or nothing of the enormous increase in the cultivated area. That the cash receipts of

Riverside alone had increased a quarter of a million in the year just past, and that San Bernardino, Santa Barbara, Ventura, Orange, and Los Angeles counties had almost double the amount of produce to sell that they ever had before, and were getting the highest price for it, he never discovered. His eyes were riveted on the Hotel de Boom, on some empty town-site, and not on the lines of green ten-and-twenty-acre tracts that were rapidly enclosing it from the outside where the year before there was nothing but brush and white stakes,—enclosing it so fast that in two years more every sign of boom would be covered up.

But the contemptuous wisdom of the tourist this winter was a great blessing in disguise. Hundreds of those whose hearts ached because he did not buy are far better off than if he had bought. For had he bought even a little, it would have been one general—

"Hurrah, boys! here we go. Nothing the matter with us. It was only the Presidential election after all, as we thought it was. We were scared at nothing."

One more such crazy fit coming on the top of the last would have stopped development more than ever, and plunged California in a depth of mire that it would have taken years to flounder out of. But people gauged the situation at once, saw that they had to depend upon themselves, and went squarely back to work. Half a million acres more that had never felt the plow were upturned and planted, on the old ground the plow-share sank deeper than ever before, and by the time the harvest of 1889 came the land was overflowing with a surplus.

Nor did the cities by any means stop growing. Though more were leaving than were coming, those who came came to stay, and were able to stay. Most of those who went away never had any business here except in a boom. The cities were all overcrowded with lawyers, doctors, real-estate agents, lodging-house-keepers, saloon-keepers, clerks, book-keepers, and small dealers in tobacco or furnishing goods, and all sorts of small fry that follow up a boom, with numbers of mechanics and laborers brought in by the rapid building of the boom period. The sooner the surplus of these went away the better, though their going left empty numbers of small houses for the wise tourists to sneer at. But the people who now came were of a different class; and two years after the decline began the school census of children between five and seventeen, and the enrollment and attendance lists of the schools showed that the permanent population of the cities was greater than during the height of the boom, and in the country very much greater. About the same proportion of wealthy settlers that had been coming before the height of the boom continued coming, and the money they now brought in was not wasted as before. Considerable money also came in to loan from those who knew there was something besides wind in Southern California, and every dollar of it paid several dollars of debt or went into substantial improvement before it finished its round.

Few cities ever improved as much as Los Angeles, the metropolis of Southern California, improved in 1888 and 1889. Its finest residences and stores, its great street improvements, its perfect systems of cable-roads, were built during those years when all the world thought—because the country had had a silly excitement—that the bottom was out of everything. In fact it was mainly after the decline began and on a constantly falling market, with imaginary fortunes vanishing every day in smoke, that Los Angeles was turned into the beautiful and comfortable city that it now is—one of the richest and most substantial of its size in the United States.

It was about the same with all the older towns from Santa Barbara to San Diego. While nearly all the boom-towns that were not still-born were either very sick or stone dead, every one of the established centers where there was ever any reason for the existence of a town was about the most active corpse of its size in the world.

And again the clamor of the brant was heard in the sky, and the "scaipe" of the traveling snipe, so sweet to the sportsman's ear, fell through the shades of night; again the sprigtail and canvasback rode the smooth waters of the lagoon, the willet whistled along the shores of the bays, the hare came out to play along the greening hills, and the winter of 1889–90 was upon us. And this time few cared whether the stranger came or not, for the country had learned that it must depend upon itself, that itself was good enough to depend upon, and it was hard at work doing it. The upturned acres were an amazing sight. Tens of thousands of acres of heavy brush were cleared off, and far up a thousand hillsides, where no one had ever supposed there was a patch of arable land, the plow was cleaving dozens of acres of the richest soil, that had lain hidden by almost impenetrable chaparral. Grain-fields, orchards, and vineyards shone far and near over thousands of acres that but a year before seemed hopelessly given over to cobble-stones, sand, and cactus; and new houses rose day after day upon land that in the height of the boom—when almost any dry land would sell for ten times its true value—few would have accepted as a gift.

To the surprise of the stranger, San Diego was growing like the other cities, with permanent and better improvements than were built during the boom. A new and complete cable-road was under way; the best street improvements and some of its best buildings were finishing; one of the best banks in the whole country had been built up, starting at the time of the decline; there were no business failures of any but small dealers and overstocked lodging-houses, etc.; and, though the population was much less than many enthusiastic ones fondly believed, the permanent population was larger than it ever had been, and the city was on a sounder basis. But to those who knew anything of the situation there was nothing strange about this. The city was simply sustained and saved by the back country, that, in blind idolatry of its bay and climate, it had ignored and despised. Great irrigating works had been built on the Sweetwater and San Diego rivers; the Cuyamaca Railroad built to the Cajon Valley; San Diego County for the first time was raising its own produce and exporting a surplus, while its interior was steadily filling with new people. The people of the city, too, had come to the conclusion that a back country was at least a handy thing to have, especially since they had it, and it cost nothing more to get it. During the height of the boom, when people were at their wits' ends to devise means to waste their money fast enough, scarcely a dollar could have been raised to maintain an exhibit of the products of the soil. But after the break, when many of them hardly knew where the next dollar was to come from, they got up and maintained at the Chamber of Commerce an exhibit that made every one stare. Within the first year it had some fifty thousand visitors, and of the lot the most surprised were the older residents of the city itself.

But everywhere the principal growth since the collapse of the boom was on the lands that had started it, yet had never had any inflation of values. Like the town-lots, dry land almost everywhere had fallen in price to a point where any one could buy it for settlement. In fact there were few places during the boom where any one who wanted land for immediate settlement, and not for speculation, could not get it at reasonable figures, except immediately around the cities and in a few other places. A special bargain could always have been made by any one who meant to improve instead of selling to some one else. But the irrigated upland, to the surprise of those who know nothing of its great productive power, has ever since the boom been selling more rapidly and at steadily advancing prices to actual settlers than during the time of the wildest excitement. More of it has since then been sold entirely unimproved and for cash to immediate settlers at from three hundred to four hundred dollars an acre than was sold during the boom—except a little for town-sites—for two hundred and fifty. Nor is this any whim. It is but a continuation of the rising values of the last seven years. Such land brings these prices because he who takes the slightest pains to investigate finds that ten acres of it will produce more money than a whole farm in most of the Eastern States. No such amount of money to the acre is taken in, in any part of the United States outside of a few points in Florida, as is received from these lands when worked to their full capacity. And no such growth has ever been seen outside of California as East Riverside, Redlands, Highlands, and several other points have been since the breaking of the boom, while some places such as Chula Vista have had their entire growth since then.

All this improvement, with the vast increase of produce, and the opening of new markets in the East, not only for all the fruit that can be raised, but for hundreds of car-loads of spring vegetables, soon had its effect. By the summer of 1889 money was plenty in all the banks, and to loan on good security was abundant everywhere. The rate of interest had fallen from twelve and fifteen per cent to six and nine, with the lender in most cases hunting the borrower.

In numbers of cases money sent from the East had to be returned because it could not be placed here at higher interest than it could be there. Though making money by one's wits has been becoming steadily harder, legitimate trade of all kinds has been growing steadily better, because weeded out to what the country will support.

Yet all this prosperity brought no relief to thousands who had reached out too far, and were vainly struggling to maintain themselves, when they would have done better had they at once surrendered and started life anew without a dollar, but free from debt. In one way or another hundreds squirmed out from under the load and saved something, but the great majority of the overloaded had to sit down with next to nothing, and ponder the lesson that a country must depend for prosperity on resources, and that Southern California, with all its beauty and charming climate, with its immense comfort and easy life, and with all its capacity for setting more people crazy than any other part of the world, is no exception to the rule. They had to learn that all such things are great advantages, but not necessary conditions; and although the climate in the matter of production is the most important business factor in the land, its true value cannot be lost sight of with impunity.

Nor were the losses by any means confined to the buyers of "wild-cat." The greater the merits of any place or property, the more certain it is to be overdone in a boom. Prices are quite certain to be forced to a point that no amount of merit will justify at that time, whatever it may in the future. The moment they reach the point where there seems no immediate profit in speculation, all buying, except for actual use, soon ceases. Then the buyers for speculation throw property back upon the market, and those who have not paid for it in full are especially crazy to sell so as to get out. A break is inevitable without regard to the real merits. And so it was here. Those who confined their purchases to the best inside city property, but had bought it on a part payment, fared little better than the buyers of outside "wild-cat."

Vainly the great majority of the overloaded tried to sell. Nearly all buying was now limited to productive acres, which were exactly what the vast majority of the speculators did not have. Nearly all attempts to sell town-lots failed when it came to closing a trade, the buyer generally becoming scared at his own offer the moment he saw any danger of its being accepted. In vain many of the overloaded secured loans on their best property. Not only was interest high during the first year of the decline, but there was liable to be a discount of the first year's interest, a commission, an attorney's fee, and what not, to increase the profit of the lender. Instead of reducing the load, all this only heaped it higher, and pay-day came around more swiftly than ever.

One by one the roses fell, and hundreds of faces once abloom with joy faded gradually from the streets. But the love of California had sunk too deep into their souls to permit them all to leave it. They had bathed too long in its winter sunshine, lounged away too many hours in the sea-breeze of summer, slept too soundly in the cool nights, and had too vivid recollections of thunderstorms, cyclones, and blizzards to return to their old homes. Some went up the coast in search of new booms, but the majority sought the country to coax a living from the soil.

Some went upon ten- or twenty-acre tracts, and more than one enterprising owner of a whole city is to-day using for irrigation some of the water he intended for the domestic use of its myriads of future inhabitants, and from the single ten-acre tract, which is all that remains to him of his once glorious prospects, and which he has held by the leniency of his creditors, is now producing more actual wealth and leading a far happier life than when he lay awake nights wondering what he was going to do with his money.

But many more, by the time they had to leave the cities, had neither land nor means with which to buy any, and had to go farther back to content themselves with the fragments of public land that had escaped the diligent culling of the earlier settlers. Tens of thousands of acres, as good as any, lay thus in small scraps around the large tracts already occupied. They were not yet taken, partly because they were in pieces too small to suit any but those who must have a home somewhere, partly because they looked so rough in their natural condition that they seemed worthless to the new-comer who had not taken the trouble to see what had been done on the same kind of ground elsewhere, but mainly because so many pieces lay so concealed by heavy chaparral or surrounding hills that they either escaped the eye or appeared too rough or too steep.

Where the mountain side slept darkly blue in the golden haze of the streaming sunshine, and huge bowlders of smooth granite glistened above the dense green of the chaparral that robed its rugged slope, there, upon ground that a few years ago was deemed fit only for the home of the grizzly bear, rises now the humble dwelling of the man who but three short years ago would not have given the world a receipt in full for half a million in gold. And where, at the mountain's feet, the river whirls its sparkling sands amid arcades of alder and willow—there, upon a few acres of what once appeared worthless sand, stands now, beneath some huge cottonwood tree, the house of the real-estate agent who, from commissions alone, had made more out of the other man than five years before either had hoped ever to be worth. Perched upon the shoulder of some loftier hill, where lately the polished horns of the deer glittered in the rising sun, now looks down upon the world below the cabin of the lawyer who gave up a fair living back East and came here to get rich on real estate. For a few short months his soul expanded daily as the stunning reality of a fortune grew upon him, and his wife's bosom thrilled and glowed with visions of the halcyon days to come; and now, with the proceeds of the sale of his library, he has piped down the water from the spring where the little green grove of sycamores on the hillside above shows the presence of water all summer, and from a few acres of alfalfa, with vegetables and a cow and a few dozen chickens, he is making the living that his overcrowded profession and choice corner lots denied him. In the little glade at the base of the hill, where mighty live-oaks nod over wavy swells of ground clad in wild-oats, foxtail, and ivy, where the yelp of the coyote still wakes the cool silence of the nights and the wild-cat lies in the edge of the lilac and manzanita to spring upon the hare that plays along its edges, is the cottage of the man who but three years ago required a special book-keeper and a stenographer and typewriter to attend to his private accounts and correspondence. Now he finds rabbits quite as good as oysters imported from the Atlantic coast in the shell; the water from the spring on the hillside tastes better than champagne even with a French label; and he has already made more money from his little forty acres than out of the half-dozen land corporations in which he had a controlling interest and "froze out" his best friends with assessments on the stock so as to get the whole. In the dark ravine that seams the adjoining hills, where the ferns lately formed a dense tangle over the little brook that gurgled beneath them, and the water-cress and wild-celery hid the rippling water in the more open places, where the wings of the dove whistled all day long as it cleft the air on its way to the water, where troops of quails gathered morning and evening, there is now the home of the auctioneer, whose commissions on a single sale often exceeded the salary of most men for a whole year, and who invested the whole of them in the same property he had sold, and at higher price than even his "cappers" had dared to bid on it. Down on the dreary hillsides of the lower levels, or along the coast where the springs and brooks have quite disappeared and only the dark adenostoma covers some of the hills with its gloomy shade of greenish black, and not only the live-oak, but even the sumac and the heteromeles are missing, there is now the little clearing of the man who had fattened on Eastern goslings until he felt himself qualified for a seat in the Senate of the United States. And even where the cactus lately covered what seemed a sandy waste, where the chaparral cock fattened on lizards and young snakes, and the roaring wings of innumerable quail shook the air at night as they sought its thorny covert for protection from the fox and the wild-cat, there the man who once owned land by the square league is now more contented than he was after he had sold out at immense figures to the "tenderfoot," and is eating better food, raised on a few acres, than he ever ate when he lived on his great rancho, where it was too much trouble to raise a vegetable, milk a cow, or provide a hen with a safe place to roost and lay.

CHAPTER XIII.

THE EX-MILLIONAIRE'S OPINION.

It must not be supposed that those who had to eat their humble pie beneath their own vine and fig-tree were those only who never saw any money before the boom. There was shoddy enough to turn any well-bred stomach, but most of the tricks that would make the angels weep were played by men who had been for many years successful in various branches of business, and thought themselves the wisest of the wise. Many a one of these had to learn that riches do not necessarily bring wisdom, accepted the rebuke of fortune with becoming meekness, and, like those more newly fledged in wealth, was happy once more in his newly found home.

Some sixty miles nearly north of San Diego, upon a shoulder of the long mountain known as Palomar, and six thousand feet above the level of the ocean that shimmered in the far-off west, a clear, cold brook gurgled through a meadow of long, green grass between fern-clad banks shaded by dense alders and willows, beneath which the tall tiger-lily and the columbine nodded the long summer through to the purple lupin and the crimson vetch; then over a long sheet of polished rock it fell suddenly away amid thickets of wild plum, cherry, raspberry, blackberry, and currant hundreds of feet below into a deep, dark canyon that wound swiftly downward to the San Luis River nearly five thousand feet below. On each side the meadow sloped gently away into low hills, upon which the massive trunk of the sugar pine rivaled that of the yellow pine besides it, while the glistening needles of the silver fir rose above even the giant cedars whose dark, broad heads filled the spaces between the pines. Here and there in bright evergreen robe stood the mountain live-oak full of immense acorns, and the lower knolls leading into the hills were green with the red oak and the common live-oak. The mountain pigeon, with fan-shaped tail and body of burnished blue and lavender, and a white collar around its neck, darted through the openings among the trees or floated in flocks like blue bubbles across the depths of the abyss below. From the hillsides above or the canyon below came the mellow tones of the mountain quail, and the gray squirrel barked from the limb of the tall pine or trailed his bushy tail over the carpet of pine needles below it. Woodpeckers in pepper-and-salt-colored jackets and red-barred wings, or brilliant with red and white on a background of black, were squealing on the trees in every direction; and the mountain jay, a saucy rogue in blue hood and topknot, kept up an incessant racket everywhere.

At the lower end of this little meadow, upon a low knoll that looked down upon the vast country on the west, stood, in a grove of spreading live-oaks, a new log-house. The carcass of a big deer, white and shining with fat, that hung from one of the trees back of the house, the smell of wild honey that lingered around the doorway, and the tinkle of the bell on the cow in the meadow were all suggestive of the old backwoods home, where so much comfort was had with so small an outlay of money. Its owner, General Milkins, had been comfortably rich for years before coming to California, but did not have quite enough, and during the first year of the boom had not doubled his investments quite fast enough to satisfy his aspirations. He was sitting on a rock on the edge of the ravine, talking to Major Bluebottle, who had come to California in the early stages of the boom with some seventy-five thousand dollars, to show the natives how to make money. The Major lived in the next little valley, which he had just taken up under the homestead law; but he spent the morning in contemplating the work to be done and resolving to set about it, and by the time he had finished this and decided to begin, it was dinner-time. Then he spent over an hour in smoking, and settling his dinner; and by the time that was done and he had again decided to begin work it was three o'clock. But why begin work at such a heathenish hour when the next day was sure to be fair, and the next week and the next month the same? Thus he had reasoned every day for a week or more, and closed the debate by going over to the General's house to have a smoke and talk over old times.

The silvery strip that marked the watery horizon on the distant west was brightening under the declining sun when the Major remarked:

"Tough! isn't it, to have to come down the way we have?"

"Not half as bad as it might have been if the boom had gone on a year or two more until all the money was owed to outsiders instead of at home. I think, considering the fools we made of ourselves, that we are in big luck," said the General. "The boys are hard up for coin, of course; but every one has enough to eat and drink and wear. There is no such thing as suffering or destitution anywhere. It would be impossible anyhow in California. The only thing to suffer much is pride, and I have mighty little of that left. I am not kicking any. I made a big fool of myself, but nobody else is to blame. All that I have been buying was stuff fit only to sell to tenderfeet, who wanted it only to sell to other tenderfeet. I didn't have sense enough then to see the folly of it. But what a piece of stupidity! For a country that can raise what Southern California can and in the quantities that it can, and get the prices for its products that it can, to be making itself dependent for its happiness on selling dry land and town-lots to a lot of crazy greenhorns is positively disgraceful. Every man that has even five acres of good bearing orchard or vineyard is making money now, while we are scratching up here for grub. Here the country is walking off with the markets of the world, its produce is bringing the very top price and the world is crying for more, and we have been overlooking all this and trying to get rich by selling unproductive stuff to a lot of asses years ahead of any possible legitimate demand for it. For one, I deserve all the punishment I have got. And yet I did only what the great majority did, and a majority too of people who had ten times my opportunity to know better."

The Major took a long whiff of his five-cent pipe, and, deeply meditating on the twenty-five-cent cigars he used to smoke, replied :

"Yes; single-handed and alone, with all the world apparently against her, Southern California has gone through the decline with flying colors. It is all over now, and although there is some trash that will fall still lower in value, the whole country is on the up-grade again. We are about the last of the lame ducks, the liquidation is about all over, and the country is making more money out of the ground to-day than any other equal acreage in the Union. But where do I come in on the new racket? That's the question. The country right now is on the eve of the biggest boom it ever had—a boom of raising good stuff and plenty of it to sell to those who can't raise it. The money is pouring in already everywhere where the orchards and vineyards are old enough.

But where am I coming in? is the question that worries me. It looks most mightily as if the only satisfaction I am to get out of it will be the satisfaction of being proud of my new home. That is a trifle thin for a steady diet. The country is now where it should have kept itself all the time—independent of the 'tenderfoot;' for the surest way to command his respect and make him crazy to buy is to show him a country independent of him. But I am afraid that I am dependent on him yet. About all I am adapted for is selling town-lots to greenhorns. That's been my business always, and I don't understand any other work. I am afraid I am going to make a failure of farming, and I don't know anything about speculating in outside property here. At the foot of that great snowy mountain in sight sixty or seventy miles away there in the north, you can almost see a piece of land that would have made me rich if I had known enough to buy it when I came here and bring water on it from that long, deep canyon that you see running into the heart of the mountain. The money I then had would have bought it and put the water on it, and left me considerable over. But I hadn't sense enough to see it; and because the soil looked thin and rough, I laughed at the man and asked him if he saw anything green in my eye when he offered it to me for one twentieth of what it is selling for like hot cakes to-day. It is not once in a lifetime that such chances strike a man as I have thrown away there, and I feel clear out discouraged. I feel as if I had lost my grip, and never should make anything again."

The General made no answer, and both sat for a while in silent thought as they looked down upon the vast expanse of land and sea before them. All the gateways of the long lines of rolling hills lay open, revealing the plains, valleys, and table-lands they so completely hide from the eye of the careless traveler along the coast. They looked down into long canyons lying thousands of feet below and winding seaward with lines of green timber in the bottoms, and away over tumbling swells of hill and dale their eyes wandered to the broad sweep of table-lands along the distant coast; then far into the south, over intermediate ranges of rugged hills, golden slopes, valleys, and tree-clad slopes, to where the mountain chains of Mexico were lost in misty blue. Far in the northwest, over the dark hills of Temescal and Santa Ana, the broad plains of Los Angeles and Orange counties faded in the shining sea, and on the north the giant San Antonio stood guard over the bright-green vineyards and orchards of Pomona, Ontario, Etiwanda, and Cucamunga. Then their vision roamed over the vast reach of the San Jacinto plains, with the lakes of San Jacinto and Elsinore glittering like diamonds on the bosom of the land, and then as suddenly shifted to two bright spots in the southwest, where Mission Bay shone inside the thread of land at Pacific Beach, and San Diego Bay beamed like a silver shield within the encircling arm of Coronado. Then inland ranged their sight again, climbing the steps of the country from the broad basin of El Cajon, green with vineyards; then a thousand feet higher to the yellow stubbles of Santa Maria; then a thousand more up to the emerald meadows and golden slopes of Ballena; another thousand up to the rolling highlands of Mesa Grande, green with orchards of cherry, apple, and plum; and then up a thousand more to where the fields and orchards of Julian shone among the timbered swells that lie at the feet of Cuyamaca.

A strange land, where the breeze never rests, yet rises never in anger; where all the conditions of the cyclone seem present, yet cause nothing but occasional little whirls moving gently over the plain; where the clouds gather as heavily as anywhere, over a land as heavily charged with electricity as any, yet cause no thunder-storms worthy of the name. A strange land, where all the vegetation of the temperate zone and tender plants from the tropics with exotics from every clime reach perfection side by side; a land where almost every bird and animal, and tree and grass, and flower and shrub, is different from any of its genus on the Atlantic coast; where annuals become perennials, herbs become shrubs, and shrubs trees; a land where trees and vines and nearly all deep-rooted plants stand green, and the wells show no sign of failing, and the springs pour out a steady stream through periods of drought that would kill all vegetation in any Eastern State and dry up the wells and springs in half the time; a land where nearly all rules of farming are reversed —where the poorest-looking soil needs only water to make vegetation overleap the bounds of propriety, and where land deemed worthless to-day is found the most valuable to-morrow.

"Well," said the General, finally, "the boom will come again. Not so wildly as before, but perhaps strong enough to suit you. Like causes produce like results; and this country sets a certain proportion of people crazy, and always will do so. There will be chance enough for you to follow your profession and sell lots again to greenhorns; but as for me, I am quite sufficiently amused, thank you. This quiet life suits me first-rate for a change. It takes me back to my early days, when I was raised in the woods of Michigan and roamed them half the time with a rifle, and was happier than I have ever been since. I have made such a fool of myself I don't dare trust myself in a boom again. I had made enough money to think I was mighty smart, and had seen just enough booms and made enough on them to make me think I knew all about them. It is not an easy matter to get such a start in the world again as I had when I came here; and if I didn't have sense enough then to keep what I had, what is the use of trying again? The more booms you see the less you know about where the top of the next one is. They change your nature, and make you think you see different conditions in each one that will make it impossible to collapse. You grow so that you don't know money when you see it. You think when you start in that you know what enough is and will be satisfied with that; but the amount necessary even for a competency keeps growing every day, and the longer its lasts the bigger fool you become, and the more impossible it is to get out and stow away a reasonable sum. I am done with all ambition. The only prominent part I will ever play in this world will be at my own funeral. Life is but a game anyhow, and he beats it best who plays for the smallest stakes. For years I have been playing for big stakes, and when I win it is all staked on another big play, and I don't enjoy a cent of it. I am more happy right here now with plenty of time to read and hunt than I have been for fifteen years, and I don't care whether another boom comes or not, or whether another tenderfoot comes or not, or whether anybody buys anything or not, or whether the country goes ahead or not."

The Major listened in silence while a deeper shade began to steal over the hillsides below and a crimson haze to flood the long deep valleys. The air was rapidly cooling, and the mountain pigeons were drifting to roost across the deep ravine beneath with the sun's last beams lighting up their lavender backs, while with motionless wing the dark form of the great California condor was winding downward from the zenith in a long spiral line. Bear Valley already slept in shade, and the light was dying on the long slopes of Escondido; the great watery plain on the west had lost its silvery sheen and was aflame with carmine and gold, with the rugged outlines of the islands of San Clemente and Santa Catalina rising like castles of jet on either side; and the broad stream of scarlet shot landward over the waters as the sun's broadening disk dipped to the horizon's verge. And then as the land below was wrapped in a weird combination of light and shade that hid almost every trace of civilization and brought out all the wilder features in a glow of purple and rose, the Major knocked the ashes from his pipe, and with a long sigh said:

"Yes, we all thought we were mighty smart. But the only smart ones were those that paid their debts and lived as they always had before until they saw the game through. Every one that did that is now away ahead of the rest. But the fellows that thought themselves big operators like we did—where are the most of them now? You remember perhaps in the last years of the war how lots of little country shopkeepers thought themselves big merchants because they were making money while prices were all the time going up? But when prices began going down they all went to grass mighty quick. We were just like them. We thought ourselves great financiers. But we were simply *chain-lightning on a rising market.*"

"Worse than that," replied the General, with an air of disgust. "We were a lot of very ordinary toads whirled up by a cyclone until we thought we were eagles sailing with our own wings in the topmost dome of heaven."

THE END.

VAN DYKE'S FASCINATING OUT-DOOR BOOKS.

SOUTHERN CALIFORNIA:

Its Valleys, Hills, and Streams; Its Animals, Birds, and Fishes; Its Gardens, Farms, and Climate.

By THEO. S. VAN DYKE.

"A keen and observant naturalist."—*London* (Eng.) *Morning Post.*

12mo, Extra Cloth, beveled, - - - - $1.50.

"A variety of topics are presented, some of interest to the pleasure seekers, others to those who would find in Southern California means of livelihood or health. We have yet to read any book wherein a more careful and thorough résumé is presented of the climate of Southern California, a question so vital to invalids. . . . Very beautifully does the author describe the sequence of the seasons in Southern California and the flowers which sing of these gradual changes."—*New York Times.*

"Without question, the best book which has been written on the Southern Counties of California. . . May be commended without any of the usual reservations."—*San Francisco Chronicle.*

"The most truthful and interesting book on the subject we have yet seen. . . Cannot fail to awaken the sportsman's enthusiasm."—*New York Sun.*

"May be safely trusted by those in search of information on the various aspects of the country indicated in the title."—*London* (Eng.) *Times.*

"The result of twelve years' experience in that noted region. The author has traversed it many times, rifle in hand."—*Cincinnati Com. Gazette.*

"A subdued enthusiasm that has the ring of truth about it."—*Puck.*

"Reading it makes one long at once to be away to taste the delights of that charming country."—*London* (Eng.) *Graphic.*

BY THE SAME AUTHOR.

"An author who is one of the first authorities in the sporting world."—*Boston Gazette.*

The STILL HUNTER. A Practical Treatise on Deer-Stalking. 12mo, extra cloth, beveled, $2.

"The best, the very best work on deer hunting."—*Spirit of the Times* (N. Y.)
"Altogether the best and most complete American book we have yet seen on any branch of field sports."—*New York Evening Post.*

"It is by far the best book on the subject I have seen—in fact, the only really good one."—SIR HENRY HALFORD (Captain of the English Rifle Team), Wistow, Leicester, England.

The RIFLE, ROD, and GUN in CALIFORNIA.
A Sporting Romance. 12mo, extra cloth, beveled, $1.50.

"A very successful attempt to combine the interest of a novel with the more practical features of an authoritative work on the hunting and fishing of a country celebrated among sportsmen."—*Wilkes' Spirit of the Times.*

"Crisp and readable throughout, and, at the same time, gives a full and truthful technical account of our Southern California game, afoot, afloat, or on the wing."—*San Francisco Alta California.*

FORDS, HOWARD, & HULBERT, New York.

"*A brainy little volume.*" — Providence Telegram.

MIDNIGHT TALKS AT THE CLUB.

Reported by AMOS K. FISKE.

Contents:—"*The Owl Party;*" *Temperance; The Shepherdless Sheep; Sunday Observance; Religion; Political Immorality; Superstition and Worship; The Scriptures as a Fetich; Irish-Americans; Moses and the Prophets; Ancient Scriptures; Value of Human Evidence; Power of Personality; Discussions Applied; Usefulness of Delusion; The Faith Defended; Toleration and Enlightenment; Comfort in Essential Truths.*

PRESS EXTRACTS.

"Clean, clear, and helpful."—*Public Opinion, Washington, D. C.*

"A delightful book. . . . Covering a multitude of subjects with a kindly light of wit and wisdom."—Jno. Boyle O'Reilly, Boston.

"The opinions are those of a broad-minded, earnest man of to-day, an optimist of the better sort, and they are written in crisp and cogent style."—*Providence Journal.*

"Nearly every question which has attracted general attention in recent years has received a careful and unbiased examination in these papers. . . . Will be widely read."—*The Press, N. Y.*

"Suggestive and stimulating."—*The Globe, Boston.*

"Unpretentious and chatty from beginning to end, the book is, nevertheless, full of strong views regarding the greatest problems of life, and the conclusions are practically those of the wiser and more hopeful men in law, morals, and religion to-day."—*New York Herald.*

"The 'Owl party' of four who do most of the talking, are a bright and brainy quartette."—*Buffalo Express.*

"Broad in view, optimistic in spirit, and exceedingly clever generally. . . . Read with pleasure and laid aside with regret when the last page is reached."—*Boston Saturday Evening Gazette.*

"Healthful, with humor and seriousness most happily blended for the making of a book that is at once pleasant and wise." *Evening Bulletin, Philadelphia.*

"Oftentimes eloquent and at all times sincere, even when the playful humor lies beaming on the surface, it is a book that will carry light and consolation to many doubting minds."—*New York Times.*

"Although the subjects are not new, yet there is a freshness about their treatment which gives an impression of novelty, and one feels the inspiration of a certain breadth and liberality of thought which is uncommon in discussions of this sort."—*Boston Post.*

"This candor of mind, and a certain sweetness of temper are very alluring to the reader, who, whether he finds his own pet beliefs confirmed or gently taken apart and their incongruities made clear, will enjoy every step of the process."—*Brooklyn Times.*

"A unique little volume. . . There is probably no time at which a man who enjoys controversial friction is brighter than in the freedom of the club room."—*Kansas City Times.*

"Full of suggestion to the thoughtful. . . There is much humor in these talks, and we can cordially commend the book to any one who is interested in subjects of living interest."—*San Francisco Chronicle.*

"The political and sociological papers are clever and sensible, and all of the 'Talks' are so bright and energetic, that this book may well be expected to take the place of the usual summer theological novel to furnish piazza-chat for the summer hotels and deck-talk for the ocean steamers."—*Boston Herald.*

16mo, Vellum Cloth, gilt top, $1.00,

*** *Of Booksellers, or mailed on receipt of price by the Publishers.*

FORDS, HOWARD, & HULBERT,
30 Lafayette Place, New York.

"Will interest artists by its peculiar views, and the intelligent general reader by its condensed history, apt ideas of art, and graphic style."—*New England Journal of Education*, Boston.

PRINCIPLES OF ART.

Part I.—ART IN HISTORY, its causes, nature, development, and different stages of progression. Part II.—ART IN THEORY, its aims, motives, and manner of expression.

By JOHN C. VAN DYKE, Librarian, Sage Library, New Brunswick, N. J.; recently editor of *The Studio*, New York.

1 Vol. 12mo, Vellum Cloth, $1.50.

"One of the best popular works on that subject, with which we are acquainted. . . . Devotees of the prevailing 'realism' in art and letters will find in him a keen opponent."—*Boston Literary World.*

The method of the work is exceptionally candid and luminous. The thought is sharply defined, earnest, and clothed in flexible and forcible English. Mr. Van Dyke, while plainly enough a diligent reader and student of the standard writers on æsthetics, is original, bold, and strictly independent."—*New York Churchman.*

"Undertakes, in the most direct and comprehensible manner, to open the wonder-world of beauty and art to the simplest understanding."—*Chicago Journal.*

"A book that the public which dislikes art-books insipid in style and vague in meaning will welcome as a literary refreshment. . . . His rapid survey of the world's intellectual growth from the earliest times, through Antiquity, the Middle Ages, and the Renaissance, down to the beginning of the Nineteenth Century movement, is in its way quite masterly."—*Boston Home Journal.*

"Just sentiments, formed by careful consideration and temperately expressed. . . . Not large in dimensions, and yet holds the results of a long and profound investigation of its subject. . . . Thickly set with points of interest, judiciously taken and intelligently sustained."—*The Dial, Chicago, Ill.*

"Mr. Van Dyke has brought a vast amount of study, careful analysis, and honest labor to the compilation of this work. . . . As a rapid, bright series of historical narrations the book is beyond compute a perfect treasury to the student."—*Daily Graphic, New York.*

"A valuable addition to the literature of the subject."—*Brooklyn Daily Eagle.*

"A scientific study of art, entirely apart from all emotional likes and dislikes, is a very useful thing. Mr. Van Dyke goes at his work in the scientific spirit, sweeps away many mistaken ideas in regard to art, and discusses it in history as a language; or, to put it more clearly, simply an expression."—*Education, Boston.*

"A common sense work in which the subject is treated with clearness and thorough knowledge."—*Cleveland Plain Dealer.*

"The essay is ripe with the fruits of culture."—*Boston Sunday Globe.*

"In these encyclopedic times, when it is necessary to have some notion of everything, and the bulk and amount of science is so greatly in excess of individual possibilities, there is need of reliable and compressed information, prepared by competent specialists for the use of the general public. Such a work is this. . . . It is to be recommended to those forming public or private libraries."—*Portland, Me., Press.*

"The public often finds art books dull reading. This author writes with ease and knowledge, and has succeeded in making his subject of interest to all who may read."—*Washington Post.*

"Will give anyone who cares to possess it a good idea of the history and principles of art."—*Ithaca Republican.*

"A clear exposition of the principles of art, couched in the simplest language. . . . It pays to read a book like this—pays anybody."—*Philadelphia Press.*

"The amount of interesting information that the book contains is of itself a justification for its appearance."—*The Art Review.*

"A careful perusal cannot fail to result in obtaining many new and valuable ideas, and in adding vastly to one's ability to comprehend and enjoy works of art."—*Milwaukee Sentinel.*

"The work of a strong pen. . . . The book is vigorous, healthy, stirs up the waters, and will do good."—*New York Independent.*

FORDS, HOWARD, & HULBERT, New York.

THE ONLY EXISTING COMPLETE BOOK ON THE SUBJECT.

THE FIELD OF HONOR.

BEING A FULL, GRAPHIC, AND COMPREHENSIVE HISTORY

OF DUELLING AND DUELLING SCENES.

From the Introduction of the Judicial Duel into Europe during the Sixth Century up to the time of its General Debasement and Prohibition; Also of the Rise and Prevalence and General Decadence of the Private Duel throughout the Civilized World; and, also, Graphic and Elaborate Descriptions of all the Noted Fatal Duels that have ever taken place in Europe and America, and of the Many Other Famous Hostile Meetings of Distinguished Americans and Europeans upon the (so-called) "Field of Honor."

By MAJOR BEN C. TRUMAN,

Author of "Campaigning in Tennessee," "The South after the War," "Semi-Tropical California," "Tourists' Illustrated Guide to the Celebrated Summer and Winter Resorts of California," "Homes and Happiness in the Golden State of California," Etc., Etc.

Published by FORDS, HOWARD, & HULBERT, 27 Park Place, N. Y.

1.—Introductory and Historical.
2.—Duelling in France.
3.—   "   England.
4.—   "   Ireland and Scotland.
5.—   "   Other European Countries.
6.—Duelling in United States.
7.—   "   Mexico, West Indies, Japan, among the Indians, and among all other Nations.
8.—Duelling on Horseback, in Balloons, at Sea, in Fiction, on the Stage, etc.; Tournaments and Jousts.
9.—Duelling among Clergymen.
10.—Duelling among Women.
11.—Duelling in the Dark, by Moonlight, and by Candlelight.
12.—Noted European Duels (several chapters).
13.—Noted American Duels (several chapters).
14.—First and Last Fatal Duels in United States.
15.—Hamilton and Burr. Foote and Prentiss.
16.—Decatur and Barron. Crittenden and Conway.
17.—Cilley and Graves. Jackson and Dickinson.
18.—Duels among U. S. Army and Navy Officers.
19.—Broderick and Terry. Tevis and Lippincott.
20.—All the other noted California Duels.
21.—Duels among American Journalists.
22.—Noted Duels in which there was no blood shed.—Randolph and Clay's, and others.
23.—The Rarest Kind of Bravery.
24.—Duellists of Various Types.
25.—Remorse of Duellists.
26.—Notable Escapes.
27.—Pathos and Sentiment of the Field.
28.—Romance of Duelling.
29.—Humors and Pleasantries of the Field.

Every Lawyer and every Journalist must have it as a Book of Reference.
Every Gentleman should have it in his House.
No Army or Navy Officer should be without it.
No Library in the World will be Complete without it.
Every Historical Student and Curious Reader will want it.

500 PAGES, 12MO, THOROUGHLY INDEXED, AND HANDSOMELY BOUND IN SCARLET ENGLISH CLOTH, BEVELLED BOARDS, $2.00.

"Not only the most comprehensive book on the subject, but is also noteworthy for the many quotations from contemporary accounts of famous duels, particularly those of this country . . . throughout intensely readable, and affords ample material for a study of human nature under the most varied and tragic circumstances."—*Boston Evening Traveller.*

FORDS, HOWARD, & HULBERT, New York.

Books of General Interest,

PUBLISHED BY

FORDS, HOWARD, & HULBERT,

30 *Lafayette Place, New York.*

Anonymous.

AN APPEAL TO PHARAOH. A Radical Solution of the Negro Problem. 16mo. Cloth, $1.

"Audacious, ingenious. . . . It will repay reading. It will provoke thought."—*Boston Traveller.*
"Written in a fascinatingly clear style by some one who has studied the problem long and carefully, and who has clear convictions and the courage of them. . . . We dissent from his conclusions."—*Christian Union.*

"That it is written by a deep student of this problem there can be no doubt. That it will create a profound sensation and lead to wide discussion can hardly be doubted."—*Atlanta (Ga.) Constitution.*
"Tellingly original. . . . especially forcible."—*Worcester Spy.*

Henry Ward Beecher.

PATRIOTIC ADDRESSES IN AMERICA AND ENGLAND (1850–1885). On Slavery, Civil War and the Development of Civil Liberty in the United States. Edited, with a "Review of Mr. Beecher's Personality and Influence in Public Affairs," by JOHN R. HOWARD. 858 pp., 8vo. *With Portraits.* Cloth, $2.75; clo. gilt, $3.25; half mor., $4.25. *Popular edition*, $2.

"Indispensable to those who would justly estimate Mr. Beecher's life and labors."—Prof. R.W. RAYMOND, PH.D.
"No library and no public man should be without a copy of this valuable volume."—Hon. WILLIAM M. EVARTS.

"A new and valuable illustration of his power as an orator, the memory of which a grateful nation ought not to lose; a contribution to the history of the nation in its most critical period."—*Christian Union.*

BEECHER AS A HUMORIST. Anecdotes and Excerpts of Wit and Humor from his works. Compiled by ELEANOR KIRK. 16mo. Vellum cloth, $1.00.

"Extracts which now please the intellect, and now tickle the fancy into merriment, but which never fail to touch the heart of some eternal truth."—*Providence Journal.*

"Hundreds of themes and thoughts, and every one with a whip-crack in it."—*Texas Siftings.*

NORWOOD; or, Village Life in New England. A novel. (*New popular edition.*) Cloth, $1.25.

"Embodies more of the high art of fiction than any half-dozen of the best novels of the best authors of the day.

It will bear to be read and re-read as often as Dickens' 'Dombey' or 'David Copperfield.'"—*Albany Ev'g Journal.*

ALSO, his Religious Works—Evolution and Religion, Sermons, Lectures on Preaching. Royal Truths. Comforting Thoughts, A Summer in England (lectures and sermons, 1886).

Alexandre Bida.

The Lovers of Provence (*Aucassin and Nicolette*). A MS. Romance of the XIIth Century, rendered into modern French by ALEXANDRE BIDA. Translated into English Verse and Prose by A. R. MACDONOUGH. Introductory Note and Poem by EDMUND C. STEDMAN. *Exquisitely Illustrated* by ALEXANDRE BIDA, MARY HALLOCK FOOTE, W. HAMILTON GIBSON, and F. DIELMAN. *New Edition.* 12mo. Antique binding, $1.50.

"A delightful picture of mediæval romance, pure in tone, and painted with a delicacy of stroke and vividness of coloring obtained in few modern compositions. The make-up of the book is in harmony with its charming contents."—*The Nation.*

"Entirely unique and very beautiful .... —*Chicago Journal.*"

William Cullen Bryant.

Family Library of Poetry and Song. Edited by W. C. BRYANT. *Memorial Edition.* 2000 poems from 700 authors—English, Scottish, Irish and American, including translations from ancient and modern languages; 600 poems and 200 authors not in former editions. Containing also Mr. Bryant's Introductory Essay on Poetry, one of his most valued productions; Biography of Mr. Bryant, by Gen. JAMES GRANT WILSON; Complete indexes. *Illustrated.* Holiday, and Memorial Subscription Editions. *Send for circular.*

"The most complete and satisfactory work of the kind ever issued."—*New York Tribune.*

"Nothing has ever approached it in completeness."—*New York Eve'g Mail.*

"It is highly fitting that Mr. Bryant, who presided over American poetry almost from its birth, should have left this collection as an evidence of his influence in forming the American taste for what is pure and noble."—*Cincinnati Christian Standard.*

Helen Campbell.

A Sylvan City. Philadelphia, Old and New. *Profusely Illustrated.* $2.00.

"So beautiful and attractive a book upon the picturesque localities and characters of Philadelphia has never before been issued."—*The Keystone,* Philadelphia.

The Easiest Way in Housekeeping and Cooking. Cloth, $1.00.

"By all odds the completest household 'Cook-book' that has come under our notice."—*New York Examiner.*

"Admirable in matter, cheap in price, it seems well calculated to supply the missing link in that line."—*Chicago Tribune.*

The Housekeeper's Year Book. Limp cloth, 50 cts.

"Gives a sort of culinary almanac for the year, with various instructions for all seasons; pages for household accounts, arranged week by week; paragraphs on marketing for the various months; *menus* for the table; useful information regarding the day's work; and at the back a blank summary and outline for 'household inventory,' 'household hints,' etc.—*Chicago Standard.*

Martin Warren Cooke.

THE HUMAN MYSTERY IN HAMLET. An attempt to Say an Unsaid Word: with Suggestive Parallelisms from the Elder Poets. By the President of the N. Y. State Bar Association. 16mo. Vellum cloth, gilt top, $1.00.

"The author believes he has a theory that will account for all the facts, harmonize conflicting views as to Hamlet's 'insanity' or 'feigned insanity,' and show that Shakespeare drew much inspiration from Greek and Roman classics, while 'bettering their instruction.' He certainly makes out an excellent case, and has done it with remarkable clearness and attractive interest."

(Mrs.) S. M. Henry Davis.

NORWAY NIGHTS AND RUSSIAN DAYS. The Record of a Pleasant Summer Tour. *With many Illustrations.* Decorated cloth, $1.25; hf. calf, gilt top, uncut, $2.50.

"Simply and entirely delightful; fresh, breezy, picturesque, charmingly written."—*New York Commercial Advertiser.*

"In form it is a joy to the eye, so delicate are print and paper, with abundant illustrations and pretty binding."—*The Critic*, New York.

SIR PHILIP SIDNEY: His Life and Times. Steel plates: Portrait of Sidney; View of Penshurst Castle; fac-simile of Sidney's MS. 12mo. Cloth, $1.50.

"Worthy of place as an English classic."—*Pittsburgh Commercial.*
"Compels the reader's attention, and leaves upon his mind impressions more distinct and lasting than the greatest historians are in the habit of making."—*Christian Union*, New York.

E. C. Gardner.

THE HOUSE THAT JILL BUILT, after Jack's had Proved a Failure. A book on Home Architecture. With *Illustrations* and *Plans*, by the author. Cloth, $1.50.

'Includes .... whatever is really necessary in order to build an artistic and convenient house. ... Rich in sound suggestions."—*Boston Globe.*

"How the maximum of comfort and beauty can be secured with the minimum of expense.'—*Chicago Tribune.*

Fanny Chambers Gooch.

FACE TO FACE WITH THE MEXICANS. The Domestic Life, Educational, Social and Business Ways, Statesmanship and Literature, Legendary and General History of the Mexican People, as Seen and Studied by an American Woman During Seven Years of Familiar Intercourse with them. Large 8vo., 584 pp. 200 illustrations from original drawings and photographs.

"It is like living in Mexico to read this book. ... Altogether this is a fresh, piquant, instructive and readable work. Many books take one to Mexico; this takes one into Mexico."—*Literary World*, Boston.
"A treasury of romance, legend, history, picturesque description, and genial humor .... a remarkable variety of details .... of valuable information, alike interesting to the traveler and useful to the business community."—M. ROMERO, *Minister from Mexico.*

John George Hezekiel.

BISMARCK: HIS AUTHENTIC BIOGRAPHY. Including many Private Letters and Memoranda. *Historical Introduction* by BAYARD TAYLOR. *Profusely Illustrated: New Map, etc.* 8vo. Cloth, $3 50; half mor., $4.00.

"If, as is alleged, 'history is biography with the brains knocked out,' this portly volume may be appropriately called a chapter of *history with the brains inserted*, for the history of Bismarck is really the modern history of Germany and the key to that of modern Europe."—*Detroit Post.*

Harriet Raymond Lloyd.

LIFE AND LETTERS OF JOHN H. RAYMOND. Organizer and First President of Vassar College. Edited by his eldest daughter. 8vo. *Steel Portrait.* Cloth, beveled, $2.50.

"It is the creation of Vassar Collge out of his own brain, the advance from theory to practice, the working out of the pathway for the higher education of women where none existed, that wise conservatism and intelligent progress by which these results were reached, and the entire consecration of his life to these ends—which is Dr. RAYMOND'S chief monument."—*New York Times.*

"A book, the charm of which it is not easy to express."—*Chicago Advance.*

Henry C. McCook, D.D.

TENANTS OF AN OLD FARM: Leaves from the Note-Book of a Naturalist. By the Vice-Pres. Acad. Nat. Sciences, Philadelphia. *Profusely Illustrated.* 460 pages. Well indexed. *Decorated cloth.* New popular edition in 12mo. *Price*, $1.50. Excursions and investigations into the habits of moths, bees, hornets, ants, spiders, crickets, cidadas, and many varieties of insects

"I have much pleasure in bearing testimony to the fidelity and skill which Dr. McCook has devoted to the study of these interesting atoms; and those who read his work may safely depend on the accuracy of what he says."—*From* Sir JOHN LUBBOCK'S *Preface to the English Edition.*

"The scientific accuracy, the good illustrations and simple descriptions make it a valuable book for amateurs and a good book of reference for advanced students."—*Springfield Republican.*

"Would make a charming present to one of scientific tastes."—*Advance.*

Jacob Harris Patton, Ph.D.

CONCISE HISTORY OF THE AMERICAN PEOPLE. Illustrated with Portraits, Charts, Maps, etc. Marginal Dates, Census Tables, Statistical References, and full Indexes. 2 vols., 8vo, $5.

"We take great pleasure in commending it for all the purposes of a complete and accurate history."—*New York Observer.*

"Without doubt the best short history of the United States that has ever been published."—*Teacher's Institute,* N. Y.

THE DEMOCRATIC PARTY: Its Political History and Influence. 16mo, 350 pp. Cloth, $1.00.

"An instructive outline review of the whole political history of the United States."—*New York Times.*

Robert R. Raymond.

SHAKESPEARE FOR THE YOUNG FOLK, containing "A Midsummer Night's Dream," "As You Like It," "Julius Cæsar." 8vo. *Richly Illustrated.* Old Gold Cloth, decorated, $2.50.

William Osborne Stoddard.

ABRAHAM LINCOLN. The Story of a Great Life. By one of Mr. Lincoln's Secretaries. *Illustrated.* Cloth, $2.25.

"Written in terse, clear-cut English, and intensely readable from beginning to end—Mr. Stoddard's, in our opinion, approaches closely to the ideal biography and scarcely will be superseded."—*The Literary World*, Boston.

THE VOLCANO UNDER THE CITY. A graphic and authentic account of the New York Draft Riots of 1863, in which more than 1,400 men were killed. With map of New York City, showing Police Precincts. Cloth, $1.

"For those who are interested in the study of the late war of the rebellion in all its phases the book is indispensable."—*Boston Herald.*

Albion W. Tourgee.

THE STORY OF AN EPOCH. A Series of Novels, presenting American life, from the rise of the Anti-Slavery sentiment (1848), through the Rebellion (1861-1865) to the end of the Reconstruction Era (1876), and on into the days of the New South and its elements of hope. "Hot Plowshares;" "Figs and Thistles;" "A Royal Gentleman;" "A Fool's Errand, by One of the Fools;" "Bricks without Straw" (*Illustrated*, $1.50 per vol.); "John Eax and Other Stories of the New South;" "Black Ice" ($1.25 per vol.). Of the 7 vols., *three* depict life at the North, and *four* at the South. The Set (boxed), $10.

AN APPEAL TO CÆSAR. Advocating National Aid to Education throughout the States, in proportion to illiteracy and to the local efforts to remedy it. Diagrams and Tables. Cloth, $1.25.

"Offers a series of vistas in different directions through the serried array of census figures that are simply astounding, while his keen, vigorous treatment of them compels and rewards attention."—*Publisher's Weekly*, N. Y.

Ben C. Truman.

THE FIELD OF HONOR. A History of Duelling and Famous Duels. The Judicial Duel; The Private Duel throughout the Civilized World; Descriptions of all the Noted Fatal Duels that have taken place in Europe and America. 12mo. Cloth, $2.00.

"Full of interest to the student, the soldier, the professional analyzer of passion and motive, and to that curious and omnivorous creature, the general reader.... One of those specialties that necessarily find place in every library."—*Magazine of American History*, N. Y.

John C. Van Dyke.

PRINCIPLES OF ART. Part I.—*Art in History*, its causes, nature, development, and different stages of progression. Part II.—*Art in Theory*, its aims, motives, and manner of expression. 12mo. Vellum Cloth. $1.50.

"Thickly set with points of interest, judiciously taken and intelligently sustained."—*The Dial*, Chicago.

"As a rapid, bright series of historical narrations the book is beyond compute a perfect treasury."—*Graphic*, N. Y.

Theodore S. Van Dyke.

SOUTHERN CALIFORNIA: Its Valleys, Hills, and Streams; Its Animals, Birds. and Fishes; Its Gardens, Farms, and Climate. 12mo. Extra Cloth. beveled. $1.50.

"The result of twelve years' experience in that noted region. The author has traversed it many times, ride in hand."—*Cincinnati Com.-Gazette*.

"A keen and observant naturalist."—*London* (Eng.) *Morning Post*.

"Without question the best book which has been written on the Southern Counties of California. . . May be commended without any of the usual reservations."—*San Francisco Chronicle*.

THE STILL HUNTER. A Practical Treatise on Deer-Stalking. 12mo. Extra Cloth, beveled. $2.00.

"The best, the very best work on deer hunting.—*Spirit of the Times*, N. Y.

"Altogether the best and most complete American book we have yet seen on any branch of field sports."—*New York Evening Post*.

THE RIFLE, ROD, AND GUN IN CALIFORNIA. A Sporting Romance. 12mo. Extra Cloth. beveled, $1.50.

"Crisp and readable throughout, and, at the same time, gives a full and truthful technical account of our Southern California game, afoot, afloat or on the wing."—*San Francisco Alta California*.

Tullio di Suzzara Verdi, M.D.

MATERNITY: A Popular Treatise. *Eighth Edition.* 12mo. Cloth, $2.00.

Treating of the needs, dangers, and alleviations of the duties of maternity, and giving detailed instructions for the care and medical treatment of infants and children.

"A carefully written and very comprehensive work, whose author has for years been well known in Washington as an unusually able and successful practitioner. . . . A safe friend and guide."—*N. Y. Times*.

THE INFANT PHILOSOPHER: Stray Leaves from a Baby's Journal. Parchment Paper, 30 cts.; Vellum Cloth, 50 cts.

"Amusing as this booklet is, its object is not frivolous nor even literary; but the serious one of presenting the matter of the child's needs from a child's standpoint. . . . The good sense and long experience of the most observing of the profession is embodied in a new form of quaint simplicity."—*The Independent*, N. Y.

"Every young mother should be furnished with a copy of this dainty brochure, which is as much a book of practical sense as it is a *jeu d'esprit*."—*Evening Bulletin*, Philadelphia.

Dr. William Wägner.

EPICS AND ROMANCES OF THE MIDDLE AGES. Adapted from the German. 500 pp., 8vo. *Numerous spirited Illustrations.* Cloth, gilt edges, $2.00.

"Presenting familiarly the stirring legends of the Amelungs, the Dietrichs, the Niebelungenlied, Charlemagne and his knights, King Arthur and the Holy Grail (Lohengrin, Parsifal, Tannhäuser, etc.), Tristan and Isolde, and all the rich, romantic realm from which Richard Wagner drew his potent inspiration."—*Literary World,* Boston.

"Should supply the requirement of a marked interest in this day of an intelligent appeciation of Wagner's colossal music-dramas ; and whether for the delight of the young, or the pleasure of the elders, it comes at a timely juncture."—*New York Star.*

Major George E. Williams.

BULLET AND SHELL. War as the Soldier saw it: Camp, March, and Picket ; Battlefield and Bivouac ; Prison and Hospital. *Illustrated* by Edwin Forbes. 1 vol., large 8vo. *Illustrated.* New popular edition, $2.00.

"Very correct history." — U. S. GRANT.
"I have no hesitation in recommending your interesting volume."—W. T. SHERMAN.
"I have read the book, and enjoyed it extremely, as giving such an admirable picture of the interior of army life."—GEO. B. MCCLELLAN.
"We know of no more stirring and soul-inspiring book. It is a story to delight the old soldier's heart."—*New York Commercial Advertiser.*

James Grant Wilson.

BRYANT AND HIS FRIENDS. Some Reminiscences of the Knickerbocker Writers. BRYANT, PAULDING, IRVING, DANA, COOPER, HALLECK, and DRAKE ; together with POE, N. P. WILLIS, BAYARD TAYLOR, and others. *Illustrated* with Steel Portraits and Fac-Simile MSS. 12mo. Cloth beveled, gilt top, $2.00.

"I have read it with interest and pleasure."—GEORGE WILLIAM CURTIS.
"A standard volume of literary history."—*Boston Evening Traveller.*
"Accept my thanks, as a New York author, for the work you have accomplished."—EDMUND C. STEDMAN.
"No man living is probably so well fitted as the author of this volume to sketch the group of Knickerbocker writers."—*New York Tribune.*
"A delightful addition to the stores of literary and personal history."—*Chicago Inter-Ocean.*

Remainder of Large Paper Edition
WHICH WAS STRICTLY LIMITED TO 195 NUMBERED COPIES.

Illustrated with 48 rare Steel Portrait Plates, 4 views of Poets' Homes (Steel) and 17 pages of Manuscript fac-simile.

Cloth, gilt top, uncut edges, $15.00. In Sheets, for adding illustrative plates, at the same price. Full Mor., gilt, $25.

*** Send for our Selected Catalogue of choice American books.

FORDS, HOWARD, & HULBERT,
30 Lafayette Place, New York.

Choice Works of Fiction,

PUBLISHED BY

FORDS, HOWARD, & HULBERT,

30 *Lafayette Place, New York.*

Anonymous. **A Palace-Prison; or, the Past and the Present. Treatment of the Insane.** $1.00.

Henry Ward Beecher. **Norwood:** A Tale of Village Life in New England. $1.25.

Alexander Bida. **Aucassin and Nicolette:** The Lovers of Provence. Song-Story, from French of XIIth Century. *Illustrated.* $1.50.

Helen Campbell. **The Problem of the Poor.** Stories from the Slums. 63c.

Julius Chambers. **On a Margin.** Wall Street and Washington. $1.25.

Chas. M. Clay. **The Modern Hagar.** Southern View of the War. $1.50.

Alice C. Hall. **Miss Leighton's Perplexities.** A Love Story. $1.00.

Wm. J. Harsha. **Ploughed Under:** The Story of an Indian Chief. $1.00.

Nathan C. Kouns. **Dorcas:** A Tale of the Catacombs. *Illustrated.* $1.25.

Orpheus C. Kerr (R. H. Newell). **There Was Once a Man.** *Illustrated.* $1.50.

Mrs. A. G. Paddock. **The Fate of Madame La Tour.** Mormonism. $1.00.

Blanche Roosevelt. **Stage-Struck: or, She Would be an Opera Singer.** $1.50.

Albion W. Tourgee. **Hot Plowshares; A Royal Gentleman; Figs and Thistles; A Fool's Errand; Bricks Without Straw** *Illustrated.* $1.50 per vol. **John Eax, and other Stories; Black Ice.** $1.25 per vol.

Wm. A. Wilkins. **The Cleverdale Mystery:** The Political Machine and its Wheels. $1.00.

www.ingramcontent.com/pod-product-compliance
Lightning Source LLC
Chambersburg PA
CBHW021845230426
43669CB00008B/1091